ALWAYS PUT IN A RECIPE
AND OTHER TIPS FOR LIVING
FROM IOWA'S BEST-KNOWN
HOMEMAKER

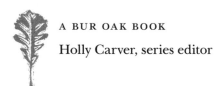

A BUR OAK BOOK

Holly Carver, series editor

Always Put in a Recipe and Other Tips for Living

FROM IOWA'S BEST-KNOWN HOMEMAKER

Evelyn Birkby

UNIVERSITY OF IOWA PRESS ✥ IOWA CITY

University of Iowa Press, Iowa City 52242
Copyright © 2012 by Evelyn Birkby
www.uiowapress.org
Printed in the United States of America

Design by April Leidig

The University of Iowa Press is a member of Green
Press Initiative and is committed to preserving natural
resources.

The originals of these columns are available for public
use in the Birkby Collection, Iowa Women's Archives,
University of Iowa Libraries, www.lib.uiowa.edu/iwa

Printed on acid-free paper

Library of Congress Cataloging-in-Publication Data
Birkby, Evelyn.
Always put in a recipe and other tips for living from
Iowa's best-known homemaker / by Evelyn Birkby.
    p. cm.—(A bur oak book)
Selections from the author's newspaper column
Up a country lane.
ISBN-13: 978-1-60938-115-8 (pbk)
ISBN-10: 1-60938-115-7 (pbk)
ISBN-13: 978-1-60938-132-5 (ebook)
ISBN-10: 1-60938-132-7 (ebook)
1. Iowa—Social life and customs—Anecdotes.
2. Farm life—Iowa—Anecdotes. 3. Birkby, Evelyn—
Anecdotes. I. Title.
F621.6.B57   2012
977.7—dc23   2012004054

Dedicated to my family,
who have provided me with
so many stories to share,
and to my faithful readers
who have kept my "Up a
Country Lane" column
in print for more than
sixty years

Contents

CHILDREN

BE PREPARED

PITY MRS. NOAH

Acknowledgments

COMPILING MY BEST columns for this book has been a great joy, made possible with the support of many people over my more than six decades of writing.

My first thanks go to Willard Archie, publisher of the *Shenandoah Evening Sentinel* (renamed *Valley News* in 1998), who offered me a job as a newspaper columnist in 1949. Without his encouragement, I may never have sat down at my typewriter and started writing in the first place. I'm also grateful to my other newspaper and magazine publishers and editors who have been extremely supportive through the years.

My husband, Robert, saw Mr. Archie's ad seeking a weekly columnist and encouraged me to apply for the job. His support has never wavered, and for that I am eternally grateful. My sons Bob and Jeff and Craig have been constant sources of subjects for me to write about. I have come to depend on their willingness to help me develop new ideas for my columns, to provide thoughtful editorial assistance, and occasionally to serve as guest columnists.

Mr. Archie said he'd keep printing my column as long as people were interested in reading it, so my deep appreciation also goes to my loyal readers who have kept me in print over the years. Many of you have told me what you have liked about my writing, and you've given me suggestions and criticisms that have made my columns better. Some of you, including Chuck and Carla Offenburger, Jane and Michael Stern, and Fannie Flagg, have helped me expand my writing to a much wider audience. The continued support of all of you means more to me than I can express.

A special thank you to my parents, Carl and Mae Corrie, who encouraged me as a child to read. Their own love of the written word and their joy of conversation helped me to speak and write well. They also encouraged me to appear in every play, speech contest, and volunteer task I could find, and that helped give me the courage to share my life with others, both in print and in person.

James Nennemann of Sidney has patiently kept the computer on my desk tuned up and running. I have deeply appreciated his good humor, technical wizardry, and ability to guide me out of my technological befuddlements.

Thanks also to Kären Mason, curator of the University of Iowa Women's Archives, who helped digitize sixty years of my columns and made them available to the public via the internet. This wonderful resource certainly helped me with my own research of my past writing.

Finally, my warmest appreciation to the University of Iowa Press and series editor Holly Carver for publishing my earlier books, *Neighboring on the Air* and *Up a Country Lane Cookbook*, for all of her friendship and encouragement through the years, and for her faith that helped this collection of newspaper columns find a place on the University of Iowa Press bookshelf.

Times Have Changed

I'M SITTING AT MY DESK early in the morning looking out at a beautiful day in Sidney, Iowa. Morning has always been my most creative time when I love to be tucked into my cozy office with lots of work to do.

My current writing space is far different from where this column began more than sixty years ago.

It was on a cold, drizzly day in November of 1949 when I walked into the *Shenandoah Evening Sentinel* office to see publisher Willard Archie about an ad he had printed in the paper that week.

My husband Robert had spotted the ad in which Mr. Archie explained that he was looking for a woman to write a weekly column for the paper, preferably a farm wife. Would anyone interested please apply?

Robert and I were living on a small farm south of Farragut with one two-and-a-half-year-old child and another due in about six weeks, so I was busy. When Robert read the ad, he came out into the kitchen where I was doing the dishes and said these prophetic words, "Evelyn, that is something you can do. Go apply."

After several days of listening to me sputter ineffectually that I had never written anything but college assignments, was a poor speller, and wouldn't have time to take on such a task, Robert pulled the old Royal typewriter out of the cupboard, put it on the card table with several sheets of paper, pulled up the chair, and insisted that I sit down and see what I could put on paper.

Once I had written that embryo column, Robert put my hat on my head (that dates this report), placed the sheets of paper with that simple column in my hand, and gently pushed me out the door. With faith only in the words he spoke, "You can do it," I drove down the lane and made my way along the country roads to Shenandoah.

Mr. Archie was kind. He took what I had written, said he had two other applicants and thought the best solution was to print them all and see what the readers' reaction would be. He also said something to the effect that I should send in something every week and as long as interest was maintained he would print it.

He gave me two directions, "Always write friendly. There are many lonely people out there. Always put in a recipe. People may not read anything else you write, but they will always read a recipe." Neither of us had a clue that day that I would still be writing this column and the newspaper would still be printing it sixty-five years later.

Each week I pulled out the card table and typewriter and pecked out the words. Using carbon paper, I always made a copy for my files. I put the original in an envelope addressed to the *Sentinel* and walked down the lane to put it in the mailbox.

Even though I was very busy with the responsibilities of caring for a two-and-a-half-year-old, soon had a new baby, and helped with the farm, I realized that the mailbox was my connection with people beyond our rural life. My words went through it and into the newspaper. Letters from readers came to me through the same mailbox, and my world was made bigger.

A year later we moved two miles to Cottonwood Farm where Robert rented land and began his own farming operation. When the weather was warm, I would set up my typewriter on the table on the screened-in back porch and write my columns there. I shared the porch with containers of tadpoles my children had collected and with insects they had put into mason jars with air holes punched into the lids. Sometimes there was a box with a baby lamb or a tiny kitten in need of special care.

Each autumn I moved my typewriter to the kitchen table by a south window. It provided a warm, sunny place for me to write during the cold months.

Summer and winter, I would take the envelopes with my completed columns down the long lane to the mailbox. Sometimes there were a few letters from readers commenting on the previous week's column.

Our next move took our family, now numbering two boys, to a farmhouse south of Sidney. The typewriter went on my mother's old sewing table, just the right size to serve as a desk. I could look out into the yard as I typed and see our sons playing. Soon we added a third son to complete our family. They gave me much to write about just by being themselves.

In 1963 we built our current house on the northwest edge of Sidney. After sixteen years of finding writing space wherever I could, Robert and I designed a small room to be my office. My minister father had called his work area his study, and that's what I called my office, too.

This study includes a wall of built-in shelves for my books and a wooden file cabinet to hold my papers. Our old upright piano fits against one wall. My desk is beneath the big window facing the front yard.

For all these years, rain or shine, inspired or dull, full of energy or with aching head, "Up a Country Lane" has made its way to readers every week. Twice Robert wrote a column for me. The first time came the fourth week of my new professional duties. Try as I could, not one idea came into my mind for a column. I decided I'd have to give up the entire project.

Robert sat down at the typewriter and wrote a column about the value of a farm wife. He literally saved the entire project. He was so aware of my difficulty in adjusting to my new life of farm living that he was willing to do anything to help me find a creative outlet above and beyond the daily work. The second time my husband wrote the column was after the birth of our son Bob, the first week of January 1950.

The Royal typewriter served me well for another twenty years. Then, in 1985, I replaced it with my first computer. Now I copied my column onto a disk, sealed it into an envelope, and walked it down the lane to the mailbox to start its journey to Shenandoah to the newspaper, now known as the *Valley News*. Instead of a carbon paper copy for my file, I saved a draft of each column on my computer hard drive.

A quarter of a century later, I'm on my fifth computer upgrade. The mailbox at the end of the long lane that led from our small green house to the narrow county road is all but forgotten as I send my column to the *Valley News* over the internet.

Like our mailboxes of old, though, my computer has become one of my links with the larger world.

I look forward to each morning when I pour a cup of fresh coffee, settle into my study, and turn on the computer. Soon I am receiving emails from friends and family. I'm researching subjects of interest and keeping up on events around the globe as they are happening.

Most of all, I look forward to writing my column. It is as familiar to me as this little room, and it is still a wonderful way to stay connected with so many people and with fresh ideas beyond the end of our lane.

I am very happy to bring you this book of my favorite columns.

BOYCE · COR. PARKE & SALE STS. TUSCOLA, ILL.

Looking Back

My First Column, November 24, 1949

LIFE ON THE FARM has certainly stopped being a seasonal type of activity. I'm beginning to suspect that it has always been an ugly rumor that farmers tucked away the last bushel of corn and then settled down to the life of Riley until the spring planting started. Unless the man is nearing retirement age or has inherited a fine fortune from his father, I know of no farmers in this vicinity who are fortunate enough to take a long breather come winter. Now that our last ear of corn is safely sheltered, the man of the house (and farm lot) is busily occupied in fixing the fences, buildings, and various pieces of equipment that were so woefully neglected during the furiously busy days of the past few months. Wintering livestock is a task in itself . . . and even the hour before bedtime is crammed full of study into the various nutritive values of different feeds and feed mixtures.

The most interesting person I met all week was a lovely elderly lady in the yard goods section of a big department store in the city. I was buying some colorful print material, just made for tea aprons, when she remarked that she was also interested in making bazaar items. It seems that every woman's church group in the country is up to its collective ears getting ready for the big annual money-making event which precedes Christmas. We exchanged all sorts of interesting ideas on bazaar booths while the rush of modern business continued to bustle around us. I'm sure she enjoyed as much as I the feeling of friendliness and working together which two strangers feel, all because of a yard of red gingham.

I spent the most enjoyable Sunday evening I've had for a long time last night reading Bess Streeter Aldrich's Collection of stories compiled under the title *Journey into Christmas*. It is the kind of book every family should read and reread each Christmas. She has really captured the secret of our midwestern Christmas spirit from the early pioneer days, of which Miss Aldrich writes so convincingly, up to the problems and situations which make our own Christmas sometimes involved and usually so wonderful. It is a book aptly named, for I truly took a journey into Christmas along with the folks who walked through the pages of this fine collection.

This week has been a busy one. Our "country club" met with its usual relaxed good humor. I have often felt that its greatest value was to give the farm wives a chance to just sit for two afternoons a month. "Just sitting" is almost a luxury to me anymore. Perhaps chasing after a two-and-one-half-year-old has made more difference in my sitting time than any other piece of activity in a crowded day. But getting back to our country club, we found ourselves far too imbued with the Christmas spirit to be content to do nothing creative toward sharing our own good fortune. So to the thread and the needle we flew and soon had the beginning of a Christmas prepared for a needy family in the neighborhood. Doing something for those near at hand is a good exercise in the Christian spirit. Sometimes it is far easier to send a box to the poor in India than to the family just down the road. It will be interesting to see how our basket of clothing gifts will grow during the coming weeks.

One of the good old country customs I hope will never be abandoned is that of sharing recipes. If I can listen hard enough and long enough, I'm sure the secrets of the fine cooks in our neighborhood will some day make a good cook out of me. Baking mixes are fine for busy days and new brides, but the fun of going into the kitchen and getting my hands (literally) into some new recipe will always transcend the value of the time saved in the "open-the-box-dump-in-the-bowl" method. The following drop cookie recipe is one that has been handed down for several generations in the Raymond family and is by far the best recipe I have found for this type of cookie. This is the way they gave the recipe to me.

Raymond's Chocolate Drop Cookie

1 cup brown sugar

½ cup butter (or part shortening)

1 beaten egg

3 tablespoons cocoa

3 tablespoons hot water

2 cups all-purpose flour

¼ teaspoon baking powder

½ cup nutmeats

Cream brown sugar and butter. Add egg. Dissolve cocoa in hot water (this amount may be increased if your family likes lots of chocolate flavor, or 1 to 2 squares of melted chocolate may be used instead). Add cocoa to the above mixture. Measure flour into the sifter (do not sift before measuring). Add baking powder.

Sift together and add to mixture alternately with nutmeats. Chill and drop by teaspoons on a greased cookie sheet. Bake for 10 minutes in a 400-degree oven.

These are good frosted with any kind of frosting. The Raymonds use the following easy frosting.

½ cup cream or half-and-half

1 heaping tablespoon cocoa

½ cup brown sugar, packed

Mix together: cream or half-and-half, cocoa, and brown sugar. Bring to a boil and stir until all the sugar is dissolved. Remove from the stove and sift in confectioner's sugar until it is of the right consistency to spread. Flavoring may be added if desired.

My fresh batch of Raymond's Cookies just came out of the oven, so I'll finish frosting them in time for a hungry farmer and a famished little girl to see that the number is rapidly diminished before suppertime.

A Tune from a Music Box

THE TINY MUSIC BOX in the jewelry store was delicately fashioned with inlaid bits of wood intricately placed in a geometric design. Gold braid glittered along the edge and down the side as bright as a bit of sunlight. When the lid was opened the tinkling sound added note upon note until the melody came through clear and bright. I gasped as I recognized the tune: "Listen to the Mockingbird." Suddenly I was no longer mentally in a jewelry store but deep inside a feather bed listening to this same melody on a full-sized music box.

That feather bed and the music box belonged to my maternal grandmother, Mary Dragoo. When I was a child, many of our summer vacations were spent in the small Illinois town of Murdock where Grandma Dragoo made her home. The large guest bedroom in Grandma's house was my favorite place to play. Here stood a great bed with a high carved walnut headboard. On the bed rested a tremendous feather bed, thick and fluffy. I was not allowed to run and jump onto the bed, but I could manage, without fear of a scolding, to give a little hop and push myself into its depths enough to be completely submerged in soft down. Here, far away from the world of ordinary people, I could dream of being a princess in a great castle or a courageous explorer on a desert island.

The music box was my companion on such excursions. It stood on top of a marble-topped table, carefully protected by one of Grandma's hand embroidered doilies. The musical disks were huge rounds of shiny gold-colored metal with tiny holes punched at irregular intervals. After cranking the machine carefully, I would place a disk on the spindle, and clamp the arm down to keep it in place. I'd push a small lever to start it in motion. Around and around the disk went catching tiny prongs of metal in the holes to produce what I thought was the most ethereal music in all creation.

Since "Listen to the Mockingbird" was my favorite, I played it repeatedly. Teenagers of today did not originate the habit of playing special records over and over; this has been done for generations.

Fortunately for me, Grandma Dragoo was an extremely patient person. All one had to do was look into her deep blue eyes to see their kindness and quiet wisdom and, most of all, patience. She was a very tiny woman, not much over five feet tall. Her gray hair was pulled up on top of her head in a bun. Her face was small and wrinkled and reflected the strenuous work of caring for a large family and facing trials and tragedies.

I cannot remember Grandma in anything except a long, full dress. The top was plain with buttons down the front. A tiny white collar framed her neck and white cuffs at the bottom of the long sleeves encircled her wrists. The skirt was gathered in soft folds around her waist and fell almost to the floor.

I can see Grandma in my mind's eye as she bustled about in her kitchen with quick, decisive motions. She was the queen of her domain in spite of her small stature. Her pantry was the place where she put together flaky pie crusts, light biscuits, and delicate cakes. As I think of it now, that pantry was a most inconvenient work area, but it was filled with a variety of interesting pots and pans and the delightful smells of spices and flavorings.

The kitchen was large. A huge black coal range stood at one side of the room just next to the pantry door. On the other wall was the sink—low, oblong, and lined with tin. A hand pump provided the water.

Next to the kitchen was the dining room, which held a large rectangular table covered, always, with a white linen cloth. This table had the great virtue of always holding food of some kind. Fresh butter churned in the kitchen and molded in pretty smooth mounds, thick cream skimmed from the top of milk in a crock, crispy fried chicken, thick gravy, and loaf after loaf of fine textured homemade bread were among the delicious array of foods Grandma produced for our enjoyment.

My sister and I always had to help redd up the table following a meal. (Redd is an old-fashioned term that means "to put in order.") The cream, butter, and milk went down into the cool cellar, but I can remember most of the leftovers staying on the table covered by a clean white cloth. This was definitely a timesaver, but I do wonder now how we ever survived leaving fried chicken and other perishable foods uncooled through a long afternoon.

The living room was my least favorite place in the house. I can only remember it as a rather colorless room with a few bright pillows, a flower or two blooming in a pot placed on a white doily, and a stereopticon viewer to give it interest. The wedding picture of Grandma and Grandpa Dragoo hung on the wall and seemed to dominate the room. Grandma had been such a pretty girl when she married. Grandpa, called "General" because of his military bearing and direct manner, looked stern. That picture always made me feel a bit uncomfortable, as though Grandpa, who had died when I was too young to remember him, was really seeing me with those sharp eyes of his and had spotted all the imperfections in my young soul!

The last time I saw Grandma, she was in bed in the small side bedroom which had been hers for the years she lived after Grandpa's death. She looked frail and tiny under the patchwork coverlet, but her eyes were patient and kind as always, and she looked calm and serene. When we said goodbye and started on our trip back to Iowa, we all knew we would not see Grandma alive again. But somehow, I knew that all the really important parts of the life we had shared with her would go with us. So it was that when I heard the tune on the little music box in the jewelry store, I knew my feelings had been correct. Grandma and her home and the joy we shared are still very much a part of my life.

Grandma Dragoo's Attic

WHEN THE FOOD STORAGE area was built behind Grandma Dragoo's house, it became far more than just a hole dug in the ground and rounded over the top with a cool earth roof like many caves of that day. It was more like a basement with square brick sides and a flat ceiling, which in turn became the floor for a large storage room overhead. Goodness knows the upstairs would have been big enough to convert into a fine one-room apartment. Only the tiny town of Murdock, Illinois, where my maternal grandparents lived, was blessed with old houses and no one was interested in apartments of any kind. Constructing such a fruit cellar and storage attic in a separate building today would be an expensive process, but Grandma luxuriated in her fine storage space and the grandchildren shared her joy.

Part of the fun I had as a child when we visited Grandma was playing in that attic. The very fact that it was separated from the house made it private and mysterious. From the boxes of old clothes, I resurrected the styles of glorious days long gone. What fine ladies my sister and I and our friends became with the long full-skirted dresses, the ruffled blouses, and the sweeping plume-trimmed hats. With such regalia we became Presidents' wives, actresses, world travelers, and rich mamas who were forever leaving the children with nursemaids and going off to fancy social affairs.

Our "children" were increased, and greatly enhanced, by the addition of some of Grandma's old-fashioned dolls. The hand-sewn rag dolls were as precious as the china-headed ones of which we had to be extra careful. Our own familiar children were somewhat neglected in the care of these old "newcomers."

Discarded furniture abounded in the attic and provided the setting for any and all of our imaginative hours. When we were small we just played house, or hospital, or church. As we grew older, our imagery broadened, the room became the setting for original plays, and the furniture adapted perfectly to any situation we demanded from it. It was hard to understand why Grandma had put such precious items in the storage room. Of course, the table had a crooked leg, but it made a perfect pulpit. The couch was lumpy and sagged in the middle, but we could not be annoyed by such trifles. The value of such treasures increased with use.

Perhaps the most fun in Grandma's attic came from the big boxes of books, magazines, and discarded papers. We found hour upon hour of fun in just one box of old catalogues. Cutting out the pictures of dresses of long ago, along with the furniture and accessories to make paper doll families, could fill days with happy activity.

The magazines were fun to look through, as were the books, but here we usually stopped the quiet pursuit of sedentary pleasure and proceeded to lug them to the shelves of the wobbly bookcase to create a bookstore. Our only limit in items for the shop was the bottom of the book boxes. It never dawned on us that putting back the books would not be nearly as much fun as taking them out. That time was a long way off, like the day before we needed to get ready to return to our own home.

Old-fashioned as they may be now, just as it was when I was young, a well-stocked attic can be a joyous place for happy hours of childhood play.

Aunt Lena and Uncle Lute

A PART OF MY CHILDHOOD slipped away last week. It was a portion that was all tied up with apple orchards and bee hives, Persian cats and a weather-beaten barn, erector sets and fried chicken, and a tiny white country church and bicycle rides down a country road.

The setting for these childhood memories was the tiny town of Murdock in east central Illinois, population less than one hundred. My mother. Mae Dragoo, was raised on a farm near this community. Later, my Grandpa and Grandma Dragoo moved into town, and we visited there almost every summer of my childhood.

The most exciting part of those summer trips was going out to Uncle Lute and Aunt Lena (Dragoo) Clay's farm home just two miles south of Murdock. (Aunt Lena was my mother's youngest sister.) The youngest of the Clays' three children was a son, Lloyd Wayne, just one year older than I. Many were the hours the two of us spent climbing in the fruit orchard and in the barn, riding on the patient horses, watching entranced as Uncle Lute removed honey from the bee hives, and arguing wildly over Lloyd's precious erector set. He didn't like to have anyone else play with the intricate pieces, so naturally, I wanted to.

My memory is sharp when I see again in my mind the meals Aunt Lena prepared. On her glowing black coal range she cooked chicken and noodles, thick gravies, home-cured hams, tasty pies, and light burnt sugar cake (one of her specialties). Thick yellow cream, pats of hand-churned butter, golden biscuits, and Uncle Lute's delicious honey were laid out on the table. The Lord may provide, but Aunt Lena and Uncle Lute added a magic touch of love to every bite of food they put on the table. They shared generously with all who came through their door: relatives, neighbors, and friends.

When our boys were old enough to appreciate the farm, we took them back to see the people and places that meant so much to my childhood. I thought the high point of our stay would be sitting at the table and sharing the Clays' hospitality and wonderful food as I had done so many times, but another experience proved equally rewarding.

It happened the last evening of our visit. "Play your violin for us, please," I urged Uncle Lute. Finally he brought out his beautiful instrument that shone with use and his gentle care. Aunt Lena accompanied him on the piano as he played, and we listened to the well-loved hymns and familiar songs. Some we sang together. Even though the kerosene lamps had been replaced by electric ones, and even though a television set had taken the place of the old phonograph, the night was touched with the magic of memories of my own childhood when we sang the same songs in the same room.

When we pulled out of the driveway of the Clay home the next morning, a great wave of sadness crept over me. I watched the white, two-story frame farmhouse until it disappeared from my view. I doubted if I would ever see it again.

A year later Aunt Lena became ill, and she did not recover. It seemed impossible that her sturdy, stocky body had at last worn out. Uncle Lute wanted to stay on the farm where he and Aunt Lena had been together for over sixty years. So he stayed. Even during the cold Illinois winter he remained. Last week, Lute Clay's brave heart stopped. He went just as he would have wanted—he was in his own beloved home, and he went without bothering anyone.

Uncle Lute was one of the most gentle, intelligent, courageous men on God's green earth. He had a rich sense of humor, a great love of children, animals, the land, music, and God, which combined to give him a warm, loving personality. His earthly possessions included the farm (small by present-day standards), several hives of honey bees, a number of chickens, and three yellow Persian cats. His spiritual wealth stretched far beyond the horizon and into eternity.

In a small rural cemetery, Lute Clay was laid to rest beside his wife, Lena, and their son, Lloyd Wayne, who had preceded them both. No one at the service that day knew that a large portion of my childhood was buried with him.

The Old Buffet

ONE OF THE FAVORITE pieces of furniture in my home as I was growing up was the ornate, glass-fronted buffet that always stood in our dining room. Its location changed often, as our Methodist minister family moved frequently, but that buffet remained the same no matter in which new community or in which different house it was located.

That buffet was one of the earliest pieces of furniture purchased by my parents, Carl Corrie and Mae Dragoo. They were married September 4, 1907, and for the first year lived in Talmo, Kansas, where Dad served a mission parish, so I would guess they didn't have much furniture of their own until the two returned to Illinois to a regular church appointment. By 1914 they lived in Fairmont, Illinois, and had a daughter, my sister Ruth, and probably by then owned the buffet.

In 1914, to add to its beauty, Dad bought a lovely set of china for mother on their seventh wedding anniversary. Mother always called it Bavarian Haviland china, but the back reads Thomas—Bavaria. This delicate set of dishes with its small pink roses and dainty green leaves, is irreplaceable, for soon after Dad bought the set, the manufacturing plant where it was made was destroyed during a World War I bombing raid. The plant was never rebuilt, and the dishes were not made again.

Those dishes found a perfect home in my parent's buffet, for it had shelves sheltered by curved glass doors, and the china shown through the glass along with a dainty set of mother's etched glass goblets.

In those earlier days, farmers would bring their stock trucks to gather up the belongings of a new minister assigned to their church. So that buffet had many interesting travels from one parish to another. It went from Fairmont, to Chatham (where my parents lived when I was born), then to Winchester, all in Illinois. It made the long trip to Iowa, probably by train, where it resided first in the parsonage in Madrid, then in Dexter, Prairie City, Waukee, Sidney, and Farragut.

After Dad's death in Farragut in 1942, mother moved up with me to Tripoli, Iowa, where I was teaching third grade. Her new son-in-law, Oliver Bricker (my sister's husband), helped with that move with his farm truck. In just three months, the buffet, Mother, and I moved again when I became the Director of Religious Education in the Grace United Methodist church in Waterloo. (I often wondered what the buffet thought of all those moves, but it never said. Mother, in contrast, had a lot to say.)

When I went to Chicago to work as Youth Director in the First Methodist Church, Mother decided to move to Shenandoah. She and the buffet probably sighed with relief, for now they might be permitted to stay. But it was not to be. Mother opted, at the age of eighty, to go to Wesley Acres retirement home in Des Moines and, yes, one of the pieces of furniture she took to furnish her room in that friendly place was her buffet. By this time I was married and living in the Farragut area, and Mother lovingly gave me her precious set of pink rose dishes.

So it was that the buffet stayed in Mother's possession from the time she and my father purchased it until her death.

Now my son, her grandson Jeff, has the old buffet placed in his sunny dining room in Missoula, Montana, where it happily blends in with his Mission-style furniture. He has placed green candle holders with berry-red candles on the two little side shelves. He will light the wicks frequently and think of his Grandmother Corrie and all she meant to him during his growing up years. It contains precious memories and is a symbol of the solid foundation of our family in the past.

How I wish the old buffet could talk and tell us its side of the story.

My Father's Background

IT IS A PICTURE of a tall laughing bearded man. It is a cow's horn with carvings done by the careful hand of a serious craftsman. A New Testament with a faded name on the fly leaf and a yellow newspaper clipping which states that T. N. Corrie, one of the best known and loved citizens of the community, a man who commended admiration and respect of all who knew him, had died after a few days' illness. These are all the visible remembrances in our home of the life of my grandfather, Thomas Newton Corrie, but the influences he lovingly exerted are still a part of every one of us who were, even in a small way, a part of his family.

My great grandfather, William Corrie, came from Scotland and settled in eastern Illinois near the town of Mt. Carmel. Traveling with him, along with the rest of his family, was his eight-year-old son, Thomas Newton (who became my grandfather). When Thomas Newton was old enough, his father gave him a parcel of ground for his own farm. Here he brought his bride, Nancy Edmondson, and they started their family. Five children were born in that farmhouse — my father Carl Milford Corrie, born in 1881, was their fifth child. In 1886 my grandpa, Thomas Newton, with the wanderlust that affected many in those days, packed up his family in a covered wagon and moved to western Kansas near the town of Isabel. Here they added their last child, Frank.

Thomas prepared a sod dugout, in which the father, mother, four boys, and one girl could live during the coming winter. (Frank was born after the move to Kansas to complete their family.)

The following summer, along with the work of turning the sod and planting a crop, Thomas and his two older sons built a frame house.

What an exciting day it must have been when the family could move out of the dugout and into a real home with several rooms.

The summer was a dry one. The grass of western Kansas became brittle and brown, and the ranchers and farmers discussed the danger. It was just like a tinderbox waiting for a spark to set it off.

On a late summer morning, very early, something did ignite that great sea of grass. The flames burned slowly at first without much force, but the wind came up and soon fanned the fire into great, leaping tongues of flame. Sparks kept blowing ahead of the main body of fire to catch on fresh clumps of grass. The roar became deafening, and the heat was unbearable to anything within a quarter of a mile of the conflagration.

Grandpa hurried his family into a wagon and drove them to a freshly plowed field. He and the two older boys rushed back to the barn, hitched their two work horses to the plows, and turned wide strips of fresh earth around the house. Then, they started a backfire.

Wet sacks were used on any of the burning brands which blew too close to the new buildings. Finally, when the fire had spent its force, the house and the family were safe.

A few years ago, I saw that old dugout in which the Corrie family spent that first long winter in Kansas. I couldn't stand straight in it, and Grandpa was over six-feet tall! One small window gave all the light they had. Imagine living through a winter with five lively children underfoot in a space smaller than most kitchens.

One winter in a dugout would try the spirit of the hardiest of pioneers, but the Corries did survive. Perhaps overcoming some of these and other hardships made them the sturdy, mature, dependable people into which all six of the children grew.

So what happened to their family of six children? Only two of them stayed close to their parents and made their living from farming—Brother Edgar and Brother Frank. Sister Grace homesteaded in southeast Colorado, where she married a rancher and lived in Baca County, where she raised a family of two boys and a girl.

When the time came for Roy, Ezra, and Carl to choose their professions, their minds returned to the little schoolhouse where a circuit rider preacher had come to hold a big revival meeting a few years earlier. The three brothers decided that life was too short to spend in anything but service to others and to God, and the best way they could do that was to become ministers. Each in turn enrolled in Northwestern University in Evanston, Illinois, and then Garrett-Evangelical Theological Seminary for the years of study that were necessary for them to become full fledged Methodist ministers.

They all went back to Kansas to preach. Ezra was the thinnest, the most meticulous, and the one who always had his tie on straight and his shirt tail in the proper place. Roy was more portly and jolly in demeanor. My father, Carl Corrie, was the tallest, rugged of feature, and often referred to himself as a " cowboy" who loved the out-of-doors. He had a calm, loving personality and a sense of humor that never quit. Dad, with his bride, Mae Dragoo, started preaching in Kansas in a mission charge in the town of Talmo. Soon the two moved to Illinois and then to Iowa, where he ministered in a number of communities.

Whenever I hold that decorated cow's horn in my hand or see Thomas Newton Corrie's name written on the flyleaf of the old Bible and read the newspaper clippings about their lives, I realize that the story of Thomas and Nancy and their family is similar to many people who, in the 1800s and early 1900s, kept searching for a better life. I wonder if they felt they made good choices.

Always Put in a Recipe

How It Began

FROM THE MOMENT Mr. Archie told me to always put a recipe in my newspaper columns I have been involved in one way or another with food. What he didn't know when he gave me that directive was that I was not, at that time, a good cook. Determined to fulfill this requirement for my columns, I threw myself on the mercy of my neighbors, my friends, my relatives, and eventually on my readers and radio listeners. They came to my rescue big time. Fortunately for my growing family, it made a better cook out of me and helped bond me with fellow homemakers who had trouble learning to prepare good meals.

Along the way, I also learned that food serves a much broader purpose than just feeding the body. It is a conduit for friendships, a setting for fellowship, a way to achieve recognition when certain dishes are praised, and a connection with generations through shared recipes.

My experiences with food continued through the years—judging cookies for the Iowa State Fair for thirteen years. At the Washington D.C. Smithsonian Folklife Festival in 1996, I was a presenter for the food portion and part of the broadcast team for Iowa's share in the event. I judged for a variety of cookie festivals, pie contests, and county fairs. My television appearances always included food chat.

And finally my own books—*Up A Country Lane Cookbook, Neighboring on the Air, Adventure after 60, Witching for William*—all including stories, pictures and yes, recipes.

And the stories about my listeners:

The farmer who copied one of my recipes on the dust on the hood of his tractor and then drove quickly into the farmyard and told his wife, "Quick get a pencil and paper and copy that recipe off the tractor before the wind blows the dust away and it's gone. It sounded good, and I knew you'd want to make it."

The lady who was stopped by a patrolman as she was driving down the road while trying to copy a gelatin salad recipe I was giving on the radio. "Do you like jello salads?" she asked the officer who scolded her for writing while driving. "I'll give you a copy for you to take home." He accepted her offer, laughing, and sent her on her way with a scolding.

The woman who stopped at the table where I was signing books in a bookstore in Council Bluffs. She told me that her mother had copied every recipe I had ever given on the air. She wrote on grocery sacks, the kids' tablets, used envelopes, anything handy. Then she tucked the paper into a drawer. When one drawer was full, she started putting her copied recipes in another one. The lady turned to go and then suddenly, she returned. "I forgot to tell you. Mother didn't make any of the recipes she copied. She just liked to write them down, feeling connected with you as she did so."

And so it continues to this day, a sharing of food ideas from columns to readers and from radio homemaker broadcasts to listeners, and back. Little did Mr. Archie realize what he was starting when he said, "Always put in a recipe."

Potlucks

A POTLUCK, Webster tells us, is "whatever food happens to be available, especially when offered to a guest."

I am not certain that is a good description of the church potlucks our congregation has been enjoying. Every dish I have seen placed on the serving table was planned, researched, and executed by one of the experienced cooks in our community. However, the old-fashioned term of a dish that is thrown together for unexpected guests is one that conjures up more visions than just the more contemporary "covered-dish dinner" or "basket dinner." In fact, some bulletins ask for the church folks to bring "well-filled baskets" (as if the ladies needed to be told!).

Can you imagine how many tons of fried chicken, meat loaf, spaghetti, salads, pies, cakes, and countless cups of coffee have been consumed at church potlucks? And that is just for one meal (an exaggeration, but not much).

As a minister's daughter I have experienced a lifelong love affair with covered-dish dinners. They always meant I could eat as much as I liked and could go back for seconds of something that was especially tasty. I grew to recognize which one Mrs. Jones brought that I liked, or which one Mrs. Smith contributed that I didn't. Being of the Methodist persuasion, my preacher father moved frequently with his family to a new community to serve a different church, but the tradition of the basket dinners was always there to greet us. The first thing the church would do as a welcome was to have a communal meal. Then I had to start all over again, sampling the offerings and deciding which foods I liked the best and which cook would bring my favorites.

My mother usually took a perfect angel food cake to such a gathering. Dad had to whip up the egg whites with the beater "by hand" since his arms were stronger. He beat the whites into a light frothy mass that eventually stood up in firm peaks. Mother had an eagle eye when it came to just the right moment to start folding in the rest of the ingredients. Even in the days when she used a coal-wood range, her angel foods reached astronomical heights and seem, in my memory, to have been the biggest, lightest, and tastiest cake on the church serving table.

To this day when I go to a church dinner I always take a piece of angel food for my dessert selection. If I make one to take, however, I use a box mix, for I never did manage the quality my mother achieved by making it from scratch.

Every church we ever served had a generous kitchen and a fellowship hall. Out of all of them came an endless stream of good food.

The care given to the kitchens and the time the ladies spent in them show the importance food plays in the life of a church. I recently heard the comment that potlucks are great as a social gathering but also provide a time for fellowship for the spirit as well as food for the body.

All church denominations excel at covered-dish dinners, especially in the Midwest. And the natural outcome of the years of planning, working, and cooking together inevitably results in some of the congregations putting together cookbooks. In recent years people who study social trends have been studying community cookbooks for clues in the lives of a certain area or period. As I look through the homemade culinary treasures on my shelves, I can see trends and patterns of food and ethnic emphasis in each one.

From Kitchens of Methodist Women, Shenandoah, Iowa, is one of my favorite church cookbooks. My copy is dog-eared and splattered. The edges are singed from getting too close to a burner as I cooked. This edition was printed in 1956, and a copy was given to me for Christmas of that year by my mother, Mae Corrie. Printed on the pages were her recipes for Christmas Coffee Cake and Cranberry Salad.

I love the directions given in that book for the MOM's Salad put in by Mrs. George Bird, Lyllis Wetmore, and Mrs. Lloyd Lorimor. Following a list of ingredients, the directions say, "Mix in usual way." Did they expect mostly experienced cooks to be using this book?

As I turn the pages, I see in my mind longtime friends—Mrs. E. M. Barton, Mabel Rippley, Mrs. J. R. Crandall (the minister's wife), Doris Murphy, and Mrs. Dr. E. J. Gottsch.

Mrs. A. Van Grundy put in her favorite recipe for Burgoo. She says about her recipe, "If this is not good, you are no good cook." Since it serves three hundred and fifty, you need to really gird up your loins to get it made. At the bottom of the recipe is the statement: "A Shenandoah Methodist cookbook would not be complete unless it contained Mrs. Van Grundy's Burgoo recipe. Her Burgoo suppers were famous."

The first covered-dish church dinner is no doubt lost in the dusty past of a religious festival or a camp meeting along with the very first collection of recipes put together by a ladies' aid or missionary circle. But it is a tradition that has caught on and should, it is to be hoped, continue as long as people gather to feed their bodies and their souls in the fellowship of a potluck meal.

Mother Couldn't Teach Me to Cook

THERE WERE MANY THINGS my mother could not teach me to do. She could not teach me to drive, but then she had never learned to drive herself. She couldn't teach me to ride a horse because there were no horses around when I was growing up. Strangest of all, though, was that despite her noble efforts, she hadn't taught me how to cook. Oh, I could put a meal on the table if it meant opening a can from the store or a jar from someone's pantry, but baking, deep-fat frying, or putting together a casserole were foreign to my experience.

Mother explained years later that she and my father always liked that I enjoyed reading so much. If I had my nose in a book, they did not ask me to do chores around the house or come help in the kitchen.

When I moved back to Shenandoah in 1946 to be married, after having lived several years in Chicago, Mother was close to a panic. "We need to get you into the kitchen," she told me. "I need to teach you to cook, something I should have done a long time ago."

Mother decided we would start by making a pie crust. "Mix up some flour and shortening and then add water until it feels right," she instructed. I didn't have a clue what it was supposed to feel like.

Then we made the pie filling and she said, "Add seasonings until it smells and tastes like it should." Again, I didn't have a clue!

Finally, my poor mother threw up her hands in dismay. "I cook by the pinch and taste and smell method without accurate measurements, and I don't think I can teach you how to cook like I did. You'll have to teach yourself to cook." She bought me the *Better Homes and Gardens Cookbook*, the one with a red checkered cover.

The first recipe I tried from the book was for yeast rolls. I must have been out of my mind to start with something that complicated, but they turned out reasonably well, and I was encouraged to try other dishes from the book, too.

A couple of years later, when I began writing my column for the *Evening Sentinel*, publisher Willard Archie insisted that I include a recipe each week. He didn't know that I was still a beginning cook, but I asked my readers, neighbors, and friends for cooking ideas, and the recipes poured in. I always tried out a recipe before printing it. In later years our son Craig remembered that if a dish wasn't very successful, I would serve it to the family again and again until I got the recipe right. "If it was good, though," he laughed, "we never saw it again."

Times were changing, too, and cooking became easier for homemakers. Boxed mixes appeared on grocery store shelves. To make a cake, we would still add an egg and perhaps oil and milk to the powdered mix, I think so we still felt we were really cooking as we put together meals for our families.

Today the mixes share store shelves with frozen foods and whole dinners that need only a few minutes in a microwave before serving. Delis in grocery and convenience stores make it easy for us to grab labor-saving foods and take them home to put right on the table.

Several years ago in Seattle, Robert and I joined our sons and daughter-in-law, Sharon, at a shop called Dinner's Ready. All the ingredients for several dozen main courses were available for us to measure out and store in freezer bags. In the days to come, the family could bring out one of the dinners, follow the instructions to complete preparations, and have a delicious meal that we made in our own kitchen.

I remember long days on the farm when we would catch chickens we had raised, butcher and dress them, and then fry the pieces in hot grease. That made for delicious meals, but it took a tremendous amount of work, even if you don't count cleaning all of the grease splatters off of the kitchen stove.

Today when Robert and I want chicken, we get a fully cooked rotisserie chicken that is all ready to serve. Since our appetites aren't what they used to be, we can get several meals out of one chicken, using it for sandwiches, putting some of the chicken in a casserole, and then dicing up any remaining meat and adding it to a white sauce for creamed chicken over toast.

Through the years I've been grateful to receive many letters from readers thanking me for recipes I have published and even telling me that I helped them learn how to cook. My mother, who gave up on ever teaching me even the basics of working in a kitchen, would have been amazed.

Here is my recipe for creamed chicken on toast. Simple and economical to make and delicious for any meal.

Creamed Chicken on Toast

1 cup diced cooked chicken
2 tablespoons butter or margarine
2 tablespoons flour
1 cup milk
Salt and Pepper to taste
Toast

Melt butter or margarine in a saucepan and blend in flour, stirring until smooth and bubbly. Gradually stir in milk and continue cooking and stirring until it thickens. Add chicken and seasoning and serve hot over toast.

Aprons

MY HUSBAND ROBERT walked into the kitchen yesterday and immediately scolded me for not wearing an apron. I was making bread and in the process was getting spatters of flour on the front of my black slacks and dark turtleneck. Yes, I should have put on an apron first, but I was in a hurry to get the bread started so neglected to do so.

After Robert got an apron off the hall tree on the east porch, helped me get it over my head, and tied in the back, he gave a sigh and left the kitchen. He has a hard time getting me to remember some of the useful tools his mother always used, like an apron.

As I continued mixing and kneading and shaping the dough, I thought of the aprons hanging on that hall tree. One came from the Kew Gardens near London, England, gift from my son Jeff who, along with Bob and me, toured those very gardens on a lovely September afternoon. Another has pictures of sourdough and the Golden Gate Bridge imprinted on it, a gift from a San Francisco friend, Caroline Getty. Another favorite is the red-white-and-blue apron I had made, along with a second one for Hattie Kaufman, my cohost for a cooking segment I did on a Fourth of July *CBS This Morning* TV show.

I tucked the pans holding my loaves of bread into the unlit oven to raise (that is the best place in my kitchen to get the dough out of drafts) thinking as I did so that aprons can produce happy memories. I never think of my grandmother without having a picture in my mind of her wearing a big cover-up apron over her long, full-skirted dress. I have a hunch that most of you who remember your grandmothers would say that they always wore an apron when they worked in the kitchen.

Aprons have served many purposes beyond kitchen wear. Robert's Grandma Erie Birkby told us of wearing an apron to school. Her heavy dress was worn day after day, and the apron that kept it clean was washed once a week.

I tried to find out when aprons originated and found to my astonishment that the first mention of aprons came in Genesis 3:7, where we find Adam and Eve: "The eyes of both were opened, and they knew that they were naked; and they sewed fig leaves together and made themselves *aprons.*"

Since then, aprons have gone on to many uses besides covering nakedness. Those I know best are the ones I wore when we lived on the farm. Mine were homemade, mostly from feed sack materials, with big pockets so I could carry eggs, kindling, vegetables from the garden, fruit from the orchard, or clothes pins as I went about my work. I also found the apron's generous skirt useful to wipe my hands as needed, dry a little child's tears, or dust the top of a table.

Aprons are not just for women. Men who are metalsmiths and blacksmiths use leather aprons to protect them from the molten ore. Fishermen use wool aprons to prevent the water and even the fish smell from getting into their clothes. And many a modern barbecue apron has a design that indicates the interest of the masculine outdoor cook. Butchers, gardeners, cobblers, barbers, and stonemasons all use aprons.

And herein comes another use for aprons—as part of ceremonies. The fraternal order of Freemasons, which goes back to early brick-layers, to this day uses white aprons as a symbol of the hard work of its founders. Members continue to use white aprons during their ceremonies. Some Freemasons are even buried with their aprons.

"Cutting the apron strings" is a familiar phrase for growing into such a stage of maturity that one no longer needs his or her parents. When our sons had their twenty-first birthdays, one of the gifts I gave each was a pair of my apron strings. Honest to goodness, often-laundered, faded, used-through-the-years apron strings. Recently I was getting something out of the drawer in the dresser that still holds some of Jeff's possessions, and I came across the box with those apron strings, a gift to him on his twenty-first birthday. Inside was a note that said, "You are all grown up, now. Go with my blessing."

My apron strings preserve many memories.

Recipe Goofs

IN MY BOOK *Neighboring on the Air*, I tell the story of the time when I first began broadcasting for radio station KMA in 1950. Bernice Currier, a fellow radio homemaker, cautioned me about the problems with recipes. "They are booby traps" she warned. "No matter how careful you are in giving a recipe or writing it down or having it printed, it can trip you up. Numbers get transposed and quantities suddenly grow or shrink. Ingredients can disappear altogether."

"Think about the recipe," she continued, "Be conscious of what they should contain and the way they go together. Never relax. Recipes will clobber you if you do."

I took what she said to heart, but I soon learned that no matter how cautious I was, mistakes in the quantity or the ingredients in my recipes still could slip in. Always, always, when I did make a mistake, I hoped my error would be bad enough that people would recognize it and not try the recipe as given.

Through the years I have made my share of recipe missteps. For example, I well remember the applesauce cake recipe printed in this column that did not include applesauce in the ingredients!

Another time I simply misprinted a recipe title—just two little letters wrong, but it made a big (and hilarious) difference. A lady had sent me a handwritten recipe for a dessert. I read the title as "Cherry Brownies" and printed it as she gave it. The telephone rang soon after the newspaper copy with the Cherry Brownies hit the street. "You didn't have any cherries in the recipe!" the caller informed me.

Soon the woman who sent me the recipe called. "You got it wrong," she said, "They are 'Chewy' Brownies, not 'Cherry!'" I had misread her handwriting and didn't catch the fact that no cherries were in the recipe.

One of my most memorable errors was the typo in the newspaper at a time when my copy went in via a typed page that was then manually retyped, and then set in cold metal type on another machine by the typesetter. Many hands handled my original copy before the final printed version appeared in the newspaper. I had sent in a recipe for a grapefruit salad that included "½ cup of sugar." Somehow in all the typing and retyping the slash was left out between the 1 and the 2, and the final printed recipe read "twelve cups of sugar" instead of ½ cup! Thank goodness, anyone who cooked at all would know that 12 cups was far too much sugar for a gelatin salad, even with tart grapefruit juice as one the ingredients.

I remember another radio homemaker who told me the story of one of her goofs. She was giving a salad recipe on the air that included one orange as an ingredient. She recited that ingredient on the air as one onion instead of one orange. Oh what a difference that would make in a recipe! Her listeners quickly called in to her radio show and got the ingredient corrected.

Using unfamiliar words can also trip up a recipe. I like to use the word roil—which means turbulent or swirling, like clouds during a storm. In days gone by that word was often changed by my attentive proofreaders to *roll,* instead of *roil.* But my favorite word mixup came about when I wrote a column about "morel mushrooms." It was in the spring and people were finding the tasty wild morels in the Iowa forests, so I thought it was a timely topic to write about. I thought it was a fine column until my proofreader changed every one of the words *morel* into *moral,* which is what appeared in the newspaper that week. I thought that was so funny that the next week I wrote a column about those upstanding, sinless, moral mushrooms.

So my friend and mentor Bernice Currier had been right when she gave me recipe advice more than fifty years ago. No matter how careful you are when you write down a recipe, you will occasionally write down the wrong ingredients, the wrong measurements, or use the wrong words. No matter how the recipe turns out in print, it helps to have a sense of humor about the goofs, whether they be *cherry* instead of *chewy* brownies, or *moral* instead of *morel* mushrooms.

Judging at the Iowa State Fair

WITH COUNTY FAIRS coming up soon and the Iowa State Fair on the horizon, many cooks are perfecting recipes they will enter into food competitions. I've had the honor of being a judge a number of times, and it is always an exciting experience.

My first judging experience came soon after I had written the *KMA Festival Cookie Book* for KMA Radio. I got a call from the Iowa State Fair officials who felt that since I had written about cookies, I must know something about cookies. I happily accepted the invitation to become a cookie judge. Of course, judging a cookie is different from making a cookie, but the Fair offers training for judges, and I was soon ready for my first competition.

The Fair has clear rules about entries. There must be a certain number on the plate. The recipe must be included, but the identity of the cook and his or her hometown is kept a secret so that a judge will not be influenced by that information until the winner is announced.

The plates of cookies are set out on long tables that can be wheeled into the judging room when it is time for a particular category. There were risers with chairs set up theater style for people to sit if they wish to watch the proceedings.

Those of us who were judges tasted one of every batch of cookies presented to us and gave it a score—40 percent for flavor, 40 percent for texture, and 20 percent for appearance. We wrote comments about each entry and hoped what we had to say would be helpful to the cooks. "Always use fresh spices," a judge might write. "That cookie would have been better made with real butter," or "Toast the oatmeal in butter in a skillet before adding to the cookie for a better flavor."

Most of the entries were very good, though there were some near disasters. Sometimes the bottoms of the cookies were not done or were overdone, or the cookies on the plate were uneven in size. With such strong competition, basic problems such as those strongly influenced the judges.

I also learned very quickly that it was important to take very small bites of each cookie, especially when judging eighty different oatmeal cookies or seventy-six chocolate chip cookies or ninety snicker doodles. I have heard of judges becoming ill from eating too many bites of large numbers of cookies.

After we had made our selections, the winners of each category were announced and we got to meet the people behind the cookies. In the years that I judged, I became acquainted with so many wonderful Iowa men and women who enjoyed baking. I also developed some close friendships with my fellow judges. There was Dorcas Speer, women's editor for WOI, the University of Iowa's radio and television stations. I had known Ester Cox through her work in Southwest Iowa with County Extension programs she judged every year. The food editor of *Better Homes and Gardens* magazine, Diane MacMillian, brought her charm and expertise to the judging events as well.

Another fellow judge was David Schoonover, a longtime friend who is curator of the Rare Book Collection and the Szathmary Collection of Culinary Arts at the University of Iowa Library. He is a fascinating person with a broad knowledge of the twenty thousand rare cookbooks housed in the library.

In the year 2000 David and I were judges at a competition called Books and My Food. Each of the cooks had included the recipes for their entry and a favorite quotation featuring that food, such as a quote about sugar plums, green eggs and ham, and fried green tomatoes.

I miss those trips to the Iowa State Fair to serve as a judge. It was fun to meet the cooks, to pass on some knowledge to new judges, and to renew old acquaintances. Whenever I watch highlights of the Iowa

State Fair on public television, I will look for the cookie competitions and feel as though I am still part of those great and tasty events.

One of the prize winners in the Books and My Food competition was a recipe that appeared in Fannie Flagg's novel *Fried Green Tomatoes at the Whistle Stop Cafe*. It is one of my favorites, too. It is especially good when our gardens produce many good green tomatoes.

Fried Green Tomatoes

3–4 green tomatoes
1½ cups flour
½ cup cornmeal
½ teaspoon each salt and pepper
Milk
Vegetable oil

Mix the flour, cornmeal, salt, and pepper together. Add enough milk to create a thick batter. Heat 2 inches of oil in a large skillet. Coat each tomato slice with batter, then wipe off excess. Carefully place in hot oil, browning on both sides. (A slice may or may not need turning, depending on the amount of oil.) To cool and keep the tomatoes from becoming soggy, drain in a colander or on a wire rack. Salt to taste.

My Signature Recipe

"WHERE DID YOU FIND your recipe for Hay Hand Rolls?" a friend asked me recently. "I have connected that recipe to you ever since I first heard you give it on the radio years ago, and I always wondered where it came from."

I'm always pleased when someone asks me for my recipe for Hay Hand Rolls. Many of the women I've known in my life have had one or two recipes that they are known for. My friend Emmy Bengston in Farragut is famous for her delicious creamed cabbage and her giant cinnamon rolls (Emmy's "Big Buns"). My dear neighbor Myrtle Brooks always made a decadent banana cake for social events. And my friend Virginia Miller has a marvelous recipe for baked pork chops that's so good it even appeared on the cover of a national cooking magazine. But for years I didn't have anything special that people recognized as my signature recipes.

I owe my Hay Hand Roll recipe to a neighboring visit I had years ago. I had stopped by the home of a longtime friend, Erma Faye Polk, who lived with her husband Charlie on a farm two miles north of Sidney. It was getting close to noon, and Erma Faye was happily bustling about her neat country kitchen with a gingham apron tied over her print dress, her red hair shining as bright as her smile. She was preparing the noon meal for the men who were helping her husband that day.

Several times during the warm growing months of the year, the alfalfa fields produce a thick growth of lush vegetation that made excellent feed for the livestock on the farm. To harvest the alfalfa and dry it for hay, then put much of it up for the winter months, the farmers would gather a group of helpers—known as "hay hands"—and the men would cut the alfalfa, rake it into long rows in the field and leave it to dry for several days. The hay hands would then either bale it or they would take it in loose loads in wagons to the hay barn, where they would then lift it into the haymow, or upper part of the barn, to store as dry and nutritious hay for winter feed.

Every day the hay hands worked on a farmer's land, it was the custom for his wife to prepare them all a generous noon meal. This is what Erma Faye was doing on that fateful day I stopped by to visit.

When I walked into the kitchen, she was just taking a pan of gorgeous golden brown rolls out of the oven. "They are made with refrigerator roll dough," she explained to me as she picked up one of the rolls, put on a layer of her yellow country churned butter and handed it to me. "It is my favorite yeast bread recipe."

The moment I bit into that fragrant flavorful roll, light as angel food, I knew I wanted the recipe. Before I left that day, Erma Faye had copied the recipe off on one of her recipe cards and wrapped up two more rolls for me to take home for Robert's and my supper.

I gave the recipe on my next radio broadcast and it became an instant success. Later I printed it in my weekly newspaper column, and it spread farther. I have made it plain, with white flour only, and also developed it into a seven-grain wheat flour recipe. I have put it in both my *Up a Country Lane Cookbook* and *Neighboring on the Air* books.

Through the years I have made my Hay Hand Rolls for my family almost every week. I always make large batches of the rolls for holiday meals, served along with our homemade grape jelly, made with Concord grapes from my husband Robert's garden. My nephew Bill Barnard always asks me for his own pan of rolls. "I'll take the extras home with me," he begs. Now my two grandchildren help me make them when they come to visit. I also try to have the rolls come hot and golden brown out of the oven when we have company walking into the house. They make our home smell wonderfully good and welcoming.

Other cooks who have used the Hay Hand Roll recipe have won blue ribbons in fairs around the country, including the Texas State Fair. I know that because the cookbook *Blue Ribbon Recipes: Country Fair Winners* included the recipe word for word the way Erma Faye had shared it with me, and the way I shared it with my readers and listeners. And the name I gave those rolls, honoring the farm workers in the hay fields the day I first tasted the recipe, is the same name given in that cookbook.

So here is my signature recipe the way my friend Erma Faye Polk passed it on to me more than fifty years ago. Enjoy!

Hay Hand Rolls

1 package yeast
1 cup lukewarm water
1 teaspoon sugar
3 cups lukewarm water
4 cups flour
1 cup melted shortening or salad oil

1 cup sugar or honey

3 eggs, beaten

3 teaspoons salt

10 cups additional flour (approximate)

In large bowl, combine yeast, 1 cup lukewarm water and 1 teaspoon sugar. Let stand until yeast dissolves and mixture becomes bubbly. Add 3 more cups lukewarm water and stir in 4 cups white flour. Beat until batter is full of bubbles. Cover and let this "sponge" set for an hour or two. Stir down several times. Add shortening, sugar or honey, eggs, salt, and more flour from the remaining six cups—enough to make soft dough. Turn out the mixture on floured bread board and knead several minutes until smooth and elastic (the dough will have a springy feel). Add a little more flour if needed, but do not add any more flour than necessary to make soft dough. Put the dough into one or two large greased bowls, cover and let the dough rise in draft-free place until it has doubled in size. Punch dough down and take out as much as you want to bake. Cover the rest of the dough in the greased bowl and place in refrigerator to use later. It keeps nicely for up to a week.

Take the portion of dough you took out of the bowl, and place on a floured breadboard. Knead and shape into rolls as desired. For buns, shape pieces of the dough into fat balls about the size of a baseball and place on a greased baking sheet with the balls not touching each other. For dinner rolls, make smaller balls and let them touch in the pan. Cover with a clean tea towel and let rise until doubled in size. Bake at 375 degrees for 20 minutes or until golden brown on top. For a tender crust, coat top with butter or margarine when they come hot out of the oven.

Farm Life

The Good Old Days

WILL YOU BEAR WITH ME while I go back a bit in my mind to the "olden days"?

I thought of this last evening when my sister-in-law, Ruthella Barnard, telephoned and we were talking about the cold that descended upon the land this past week. "I'm glad I don't have to go out and bring in cobs and wood and coal to keep the fire going in the stove like I used to." I could tell Ruthella shivered a little as she spoke.

"I'm glad to have a tight, well-insulated house. Those drafty, thin-walled houses from my past make me shudder, too," I answered.

It is no wonder older relatives vividly remember some of those struggles experienced during wintertime, especially if they lived on the farm. The work needed to keep the livestock well was difficult indeed. I remember the local radio stations airing "livestock warnings" that sent Robert and the rest of the farmers out into the cold wind to herd cattle and horses to shelter and to look after the hogs, sheep, and chickens. They would check the fires in the "cowboy heaters" in the stock tanks that kept the water from freezing so the livestock could drink. These stoves were cast iron and made to be immersed part way into the water. Cobs, wood scraps, and coal were used by most of the farmers to keep the fires going during the coldest winter months.

If a storm was brewing, I would check the windows of the house to be certain they were as tight as possible, then pull the curtains together to keep out the drafts. Then I put the children's playpen near the Warm Morning stove in the living room, put blankets around three sides, and turned the open side toward the stove. The bottom of the playpen was a few inches off the floor so it made a snug little play area for the children.

I often think of Robert milking our eleven Guernsey cows by hand and carrying the buckets of milk back to the house through the frosty morning air. I separated the cream out of the milk on the back porch, which had a chill all its own. But we were thankful to have those cows, for we sold the cream produced from their rich milk for cash or traded it for groceries that helped keep the family fed.

In the winter, doing the family wash could be stressful. Despite the fact that Robert put protective plastic covering over the screens on the porch, that area was still very cold. I'd hurry through the washing process as quickly as possible with my wringer-washer. Unless we were in the midst of a heavy snowstorm, I hung the clothes outside on the clothesline. I warmed the clothespins in the oven before I went out to help keep my hands warm as I worked.

I have never figured out how fabric can freeze dry, but it does. I'd bring the frozen clothing inside and stand the overalls and long underwear and towels near the kitchen stove. It was fun to watch as they slowly crumpled onto the floor like melting snowmen.

When a blizzard blew in from the north or west I hung the freshly washed clothes on racks near the heating stove in the living room. This produced moisture that made a glaze over the windows that the children enjoyed using as drawing boards. They created pictures with their warm fingers or used metal objects such as cookie cutters and thimbles to make designs in the frost.

For the houses without bathrooms, the toilets were really out-houses that could only be reached by going outdoors. Using this fa-cility in the summer was no problem, but in the winter, one did not linger long at this task. Many people kept a receptacle under each bed, known as "thunder mugs," "chamber pots," or "slop jars," for long winter nights. (If you want to see what these looked like, stop by a historical museum.)

The next time any of your more mature relatives begin to talk about the "old days," listen to them. If nothing else, it should give you an appreciation of the labor saving devices, the ability to warm and light your house with a flip of a switch, and realize that a bottle of milk is as close as the grocery store. Going out to milk the cows when the temperature reads below zero is no longer a necessity for most people.

Perhaps the "good old days" weren't so great after all.

Porches

IF I HAD THE PLEASURE of living with one of the modern patios or screened breezeways, I might feel differently, but the good old-fashioned porch has much in its favor.

When we were first married in 1946, we lived in the Victoria Apartments in Shenandoah, Iowa. The building had a huge porch running around the east side (perhaps the word "veranda" applies to such an outdoor sitting room). Leastwise, it was a pleasant place to sit when my work was done and my feet grew weary.

The first farmhouse in which we lived south of Farragut, Iowa, had an east porch that faced a wide expanse of lawn, the garden, and then a large field. It was really a private porch and served well as an extra room. With Grandpa's big hand-me-down table it was the perfect spot for early morning breakfasts, for late evening suppers, and an occasional midday meal. A bed with the head and foot cut low made a wide couch upon which the children could nap or play. When company came it was excellent for extra sleeping. My, we used that porch.

The porch at our next home, Cottonwood Farm, was much more of a utilitarian space. With the cream separator and the washing equipment it was never a thing of beauty, but we did find a corner for Grandpa's table. Many a summer morning we ate a quiet breakfast looking out over the rolling hills that stretched down to Mill Creek. When company or harvest hands arrived, the porch became our dining room, and a handy one it was.

By 1956 we had moved to the Redd Farm. Now we had a wide porch looking to the east. Its big swing made a nice place to rest, rock a baby to sleep, or listen to our sons discuss the latest in model airplanes. Gradually the porch had more occupants. A table went out for use during tea parties, for breakfast trays, and for our three sons when the capacity of the dining room was stretched too far. A small couch and a toy box made it nice for naps. The porch had an added advantage, being close to the highway as it was. When son Jeff got out of sorts we'd sit and guess what would come over the hill next—a car, a pickup, or a truck? Before long his tears were dried, and our laughs returned.

My sister, Ruth, who lived south of Farragut, remodeled their farmhouse porch into a family room. With windows all around, tile on the floor, fresh cafe curtains, the kind of furniture which just begs one to relax, it was the perfect answer to summer living.

I hope we always have porches. They have provided a wonderful service in the past and could, even today, give families the perfect place to enjoy.

Back Doors

PRACTICALLY EVERY FARMHOUSE has a front door, an opening that enters a hall, living room, or foyer of a home. But whoever heard of anyone, friend or stranger, who goes into the front door of a rural dwelling?

It seldom fails that a knock comes when the lady of the house has the clothes well strewn in piles around the porch floor preparatory to washing them. Or perchance it is a bit later on a rainy day, and the wash is hanging in wet inanimate shapes along the lines strung across the porch. When a knock comes at such times, it takes a veritable Sherlock Holmes to wend a path to the kitchen door and at the same time keep from getting slapped in the face by a pair of wet overalls. I prefer that only familiar faces appear at such moments.

When I was growing up in a small town Iowa parsonage I was completely unaware of this complicating factor in the lives of farm families. Mother always kept the rooms near the front of the house in perfect order and only the back part was open territory for my sister and my childish clutter. We knew that at any time of day or night someone might come for a wedding, to call the preacher to a sick bed, or to stop in with a news report for next week's bulletin. The living room had to be neat at all times to meet these people on their various errands.

It was a most startling experience when I joined the ranks of farm wives to realize that the entire house was under surveillance, for now the back porch came into view first, then the kitchen, and finally the other rooms in rapid succession. Only the sanctity of a second story could make any corner of the house unavailable to the visitor's eye.

This situation always seemed to reach a climax on the day a group of our country social club ladies were due to gather for a meeting. Some place must be found to put the usual odds and ends that are not needed or do not particularly add beauty to the house. In many homes the unneeded items are duly delegated to the out-of-bounds area of the back porch. Out of bounds? Not for the farm wife. (The skeptical must remember that most older farmhouses are not blessed with basements or attics.) Perhaps when the guests arrive they will enter by the front door, but come time to leave and someone will surely start the group headed toward the back of the house. Visions of murder may dance in the poor hostess's head, but out onto the porch and through the back door they'll go regardless.

My most embarrassing back porch moment came one day in the midst of a flurry of housecleaning. A big family dinner was in the making, and for this the house had to be spotless. My usual routine was to start in the living room and work the cleaning process back through the house, ending on the back porch with all the papers to discard and rugs to be shaken. Just as I swept the last of the kitchen clear and stepped out on the porch ready for the final fling, the screen door opened and in stepped three of the fine ladies of our church dressed in their calling best. Over the tops of the wastebaskets, I smiled a weak greeting.

"Do come in . . . if you can," I urged, pushing rugs aside with the broom to make a path. They finally made it.

One of the ladies broke the ice by saying, "You certainly are accomplishing a great deal today . . . at least so far!" We all laughed and my embarrassment vanished. But I just knew those ladies had never been met at the door with a more disheveled hostess.

Perhaps we need a Farm Wives Union to advocate houses built with lanes curving attractively up near the front door where the flowers are the prettiest, the grass the greenest, and the view the nicest when opening the door. Until that day, many of us will try and put our best foot forward, all washing, dirty clothes, cream separators, and stored items notwithstanding.

Cottonwood Farm's Ghost

HAMLET AND *MACBETH*, by one William Shakespeare, have nothing on Cottonwood Farm, for we too have a ghost.

We were completely unaware of this uninvited inhabitant until shortly after we moved to this farm eight miles south of the town of Farragut, Iowa. One misty night we heard a moaning and then a number of restless sounds. Another time, in early morning when a fog lay across the meadow and over the Mill Creek Valley, we heard the low and mournful sound again. Surprisingly enough, its greatest intensity came one bright sunshiny afternoon when the minister and his wife came to call.

I had just brought in cups of tea and a plate of cookies for our guests when the low moaning began. Husband Robert and I tried to lightly dismiss the eerie sounds.

"Oh, that must be the steamboat going up Mill Creek," I laughed.

"Maybe it's the skeleton in the closet stretching his bones," Robert added with a grin. But the increased tone and the insistence of the sad voice made us fear the entrance at any moment of an unearthly creature dressed in robes of ectoplasm (or whatever it is a ghost is supposed to wear). Soon our guests said their goodbyes and drove quickly down the lane.

Trying to make the best of a bad situation, we finally decided that having a ghost was a mark of distinction. After all, large estates and manor houses in Britain have their famous haunts. While our cottage could hardly claim to be part of any large estate, and calling it a manor house would certainly be a misnomer, perhaps we could still claim a little bit of fame.

It became a game for us: was our ghost some famous pioneer who long ago had been cheated out of his rightful land? Or perhaps it was a Native American of noble lineage left on this spot to die who was now seeking revenge on the white men who live on his sacred premises. Our ghost gradually became a friendly, unseen member of the family.

Was the mystery of the ghost ever solved?

Oh, yes. We discovered that the windmill made that low, eerie, moaning sound when the water was low in the tanks and the vanes were moving slowly 'round and 'round.

Canning

EVERY HOUSEWIFE needs a mathematical brain, which is a quality, alas, I sadly lack. By the time the nine-day, twelve-day, and fourteen-day pickles have their needed number of brinings and syrupings, I wish longingly for a chance to restudy my sixth grade arithmetic.

Just as I was gloating in unreasonable pride over my seventy quarts of green beans and my sixteen pints of pickled beans all processed in my pressure canner, here comes a neighbor with ninety quarts of beans, all boiled for three long hours in a hot water bath. My boasting deflated like a popped blob of bubble gum. I wonder how many of you still process your beans for those long hours, thankful that the garden produced in such abundance.

In answer to a question, "Yes, I do like to can." I enjoy jelly and jam making best of all, I like pickling next, but even the common vegetables give me a feeling of accomplishment as I put them into the jars. Perhaps it's a throwback to early pioneers or the days of the Depression in which we were raised, but to have food in the basement and in the locker gives me a feeling of security. Home canned goods help push the grocery bill downward a bit, also.

No, I do not enjoy coping with little ones while pouring hot jelly into the glasses or hot syrup over the pickles and hot tomato soup into the jars. But these same little helpers pressure me into processing even more garden produce for meals to come.

No, I do not like to clean up the mess. But corn does come on cobs, beans do come with tips, apples do come with cores, tomatoes have white centers, and peaches have seeds and skins. Betwixt the sink and the jar, thereby, accumulates the parts to be discarded. Taking the uninteresting with the exciting includes a stint with the dishcloth and the wet mop, whether I like it or not!

Moving Day

FOR MANY A businessman whose year begins on January 1, a preacher whose church year starts on July 1, or a school teacher whose contract runs from September to September, the first of March is no more than a day to tear off the calendar sheet marked February, look out the windows to see if the weather is lionlike, and pull a sheaf of bills from the mailbox.

For the farmer, March 1 is really the beginning of his year. Now he must begin a new cycle of spring plowing, planting, fertilizing, and cultivating.

Most tenant farmers, in the Midwest at least, run on a March to March contract. By the first of November (in Iowa) the owner must tell his tenant if he wants him to move by March. By the same token, the renter must tell his landlord if he intends to leave for new (and he hopes, greener) fields. This throws the traditional moving day right smack onto March 1.

This may follow the demands of farm work, but invariably it runs into complications, for the packing, loading, and hauling which are needed for such an undertaking must be done with winter still much in evidence. Farm lanes are not noted for permanent surfacing nor March for clement weather. How many truckloads of furniture have been pulled through mud or pummeled with sleet or rain? How many tractors, cultivators, and corn pickers have been lugged or trucked through ruts to get to a new place of endeavor?

It would be interesting to know how many families are moving this year under such circumstances. When you realize the great number of farms which are rented, it is easy to see that the shift could be tremendous.

Whether those with farm sales are more or less fortunate is surely a matter of opinion. Sometimes I think a farm sale would eliminate a lot of the packing and carrying which must be done. On the other hand, wouldn't it be extremely difficult to see the coffee table, which was the first Christmas gift for a new bride from her husband, go to the highest bidder?

It may be rationalizing, but it does help to emphasize the disagreeable aspects of a place when moving. It certainly makes it easier, psychologically, to leave when the cold wind is whistling around the farmhouse and the temperature is below zero than when the hills gleam green and gold. It is better to concentrate on the unpleasantness of mud and snow and ice than to dwell on the fun of coasting with happy children down a particular long hill or swaying high on a great load of August hay as it comes lumbering in from a far field. So it really is best to look at the inconvenient and the uncomfortable as you plan to take the happy times right along with you.

When we moved from the farm south of Farragut, Iowa, to our present home near Sidney in 1955, it was on the traditional March 1 date. While the chill winds blew, we packed books, summer clothes, vases, the broken lamp which would surely get fixed someday, fruit jars (empty and full), bags of potatoes, furniture, toys, and bedding. Last of all, we put the in-season and good clothes into a huge box reserved just for that purpose. We did not know until the box was unpacked at our new house that five-year-old Bob, fearful his sturdy pet might be left behind, had tucked the black barn cat into a box of clothing. Thank goodness we had only sixteen miles to go. The cat, and the clothes, came through in tolerable shape.

As I packed, I marked each box with the room or location in which it was to be placed in our new home: basement, kitchen, back porch, bathroom, boys' room, living room. When the dust had settled, and I began the process of unpacking, I discovered the box marked "living room" was in the basement, the one marked "kitchen" was in the living room, and the one marked "bathroom" was nowhere to be found!

This is easier to understand (we are literate people) when I explain that we moved in our pickup, did all the work ourselves, and took many trips to get the task completed. By the time the final run was made, our only desire was to get everything under the roof regardless of location.

Children

Dulcie Jean's Kindergarten

HAVING A LITTLE GIRL in kindergarten is an exciting experience. Each evening when Dulcie Jean arrives home, we receive a running account of school from her own particular viewpoint; it has become the high point of each day. Her complete enjoyment of all they do in school shines through every remark she makes. We get a sudden clear glimpse into a room full of forty-seven wiggly, lively, curious, interesting little people who are busily engaged in discovering the world around them and ways in which to live peacefully in such a large group.

It has been amazing to see how these many personalities, with their different home backgrounds, each coming to school with his or her own limitations and abilities, have become an integrated, workable, socially adapted class. It has happened under the quiet direction of their teacher, Miss Loree Hogsett. A kindergarten teacher, more than any other, is a substitute mother, and only with the great love and patience which Miss Hogsett has in great quantity, can she guide so many youngsters into the way of learning.

One morning Dulcie Jean insisted that I empty all the boxes in the cupboard so she could take them to school for their new store. "The people in the doll corner are going to come over to the store and buy things. I need to take lots of boxes," she insisted.

After convincing her that she didn't need everything in the house, we compromised on several oatmeal, cocoa, cracker, and Jello boxes. When she saw the bulky package these few made, she decided they were quite enough for her to carry down the lane to the gate where she would meet the school bus.

That evening, when she bounced off the bus, she informed us delightedly that she had been the storekeeper for the day. Educationally the children received real life experiences from such activities, but to us it was a little girl lugging a big sack of emptied boxes down the lane, being an excited storekeeper, and selling a box of oatmeal to the "doll corner people."

It means everything to be able to send a happy little girl out the door, knowing as I watch her go down the lane with the little kitty following after her that the day will be full of interest for her from the minute she gets on the school bus until she arrives home again. Parents appreciate (more than they often express) the hard work by the teachers who keep a smooth-running classroom and a happy environment in which personalities and minds alike may develop.

My personal mothering experience is limited to the kindergarten class, but I know that thanks should go to the work being done with that large group of small youngsters. We are mighty grateful for their teacher, Loree Hogsett.

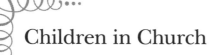

Children in Church

OUR FAMILY ALWAYS believed in starting children to church at an early age. As a result of this youthful attendance, we have stories of our childhood escapades filed away in our memories. My sister and I certainly acted normally as we were growing up, but preacher's children are supposed to be more virtuous, well-trained, disciplined, or in some magic manner, be able to put aside their childish ways when they enter the interior of a church.

The favorite story told about my sister Ruth was enacted in 1915 when she was two-and-one-half years old. She was attending church well fortified with crackers. Some way, she stepped out of Mother's grasp and went running down the aisle calling, "Want a bite, Daddy?"

My father's reaction was never recorded, but I have a feeling that my mother got Ruth back under control, and the service continued.

Seemingly, my main desire during a church service was to get up into the pulpit with Dad. Since my mother was unsympathetic enough to insist that I sit with her instead of mounting the fascinating heights of the podium, I contented myself with mimicking Dad's facial expressions and arm-waving gestures. It must have been rather disconcerting for him to come to the climax of some great spiritual discussion and look down upon a congregation which held in its center a little caricature of himself.

Fast forward to 1952 when son Bob topped the performance of all the rest of the family. He was sitting with his father, Robert, while our daughter Dulcie Jean and I were involved with the children's choir. Little difficulty is ever anticipated with this two-year-old as long as his beloved toy tractor is with him, so when time to take the collection arrived, Robert just stepped out of the pew and left Bob contentedly interested in his toy. As Robert stood quietly at the altar listening to the minister's prayer of thanksgiving, we heard a familiar "put-put-put-put" noise coming up the aisle. Robert turned from the altar and there at his feet was one tiny boy down on his hands and knees pushing his tractor and noisily adding all the necessary sound effects. Scooping Bob up in his arms, Robert made a quick retreat back up the aisle and into the pew.

Next time he took up the offering, Robert was certain his son was left tightly enclosed in someone's custody.

One of my favorite stories is about the little girl who was talking to her mother about God. "No one knows what God looks like," said the mother.

"They do now," said the little girl, "I just drew a picture of him."

One day Dulcie Jean came in from a long session of drawing pictures on huge pieces of wallpaper laid out on the picnic table. Having learned the hard way to never give an adult version of a picture's content, I said, "My what a nice picture. Will you tell me about it?"

"Well, there is a house here, see?" Dulcie Jean said.

"I see."

"And here are the trees and flowers." I tried to look as if I realized the marks and colors were the finest trees and flowers anyone had ever drawn. "And see here, these are moons, and those are suns," she pointed to some round objects at the top of the picture.

"And what is this?" I asked, pointing to an interesting mixture of lines rising from the roof of the house.

"Don't you know? That's Jesus."

At that moment I knew exactly what Jesus looks like. He was carefully visualized by an almost five-year-old through the medium of a torn piece of wallpaper and stubby crayons. Needless to say, that picture was carefully preserved with my special treasures.

Craig's First Smile

THE SNOW IS PILED deep around the little white house with the green trim. Outside the big dining room window, which we call our 'picture window,' the trees stand black and awkward in their nude gauntness. Here and there, a slanting branch is softened into modesty with a garment of snow. White drifts stretch out below until they drop into the crevasse which is formed by the creek, now iced into silence. The tiny sparrows hover close under the wide eaves of the house. Surely any of the little creatures must find the going cold and the feeding difficult when everything is so thoroughly frozen. Silver Dog stands as a sturdy white sentinel on the steps, his coat only a few shades darker than the snow.

But inside our little white house the day is full of sunshine, regardless of the climate outside, for our youngest son, Craig, has started to smile. Strange how we watch for that first glimmer of human recognition: the close concentration which is theirs when they see a face come nodding into their area of perception. Then comes that most wondrous of days when the smile that is really a smile comes to respond to the affection sent out to him. No gas pain this. Craig's smile lights his eyes and dimples his face. In God's wisdom in the ways of love, He gave a tiny one the greatest weapon in the world as his first sign of development. With that smile, tiny Craig can get anything he wants and make us all vie with each other to do the needed task. All we need in pay for the daily work we do is the unselfishly given gift of our baby's smile.

If ever an argument holds sway about the existence of the immortal soul, the people who take the negative view have surely lacked the experience of seeing a baby's first smile. Here is, without a doubt, a touch of heaven with the glory shining through.

Supper Talk

MY SONS GOT INTO a discussion at the supper table last evening. My husband Robert really started it by telling of the activities he had as a boy that "youngsters don't do anymore." He did comment that part of the trouble was that many of the opportunities aren't around: the creeks have been bulldozed in, highways have cut through the hiking trails, and attics and cob sheds are not as accessible as they used to be for playhouses and explorer's huts.

"We have some places to hike and fish and swim," son Bob said. "So many kids in the cities don't have a chance to do those things."

"I want to go to the city," Craig piped up.

"Maybe wherever people live there are exciting things to do and see and varied ways to grow and learn. Opportunity to have different experiences and stretch our minds and imaginations can be anywhere," Robert concluded. I added that from the time children are born, they need to be surrounded with books and music and beauty, both of nature and of artistic man-made design. Libraries reach out everywhere. Good music can be found on radio and television with a little extra perseverance. Paintings are on exhibition in many places, from city galleries to country fairs. Nature is near everyone, even if it is a tree in a park or a geranium in a pot.

"Your thinking is narrow if you limit creativeness to music and art and literature," my sister-in-law Ruthella exclaimed when we were talking over a cup of coffee the following day. "Take my son, Tom, for example."

Now Tom is five years old and I knew exactly what Ruthella meant. She never knows when he gets up in the morning if he will be Superman, a railroad engineer, or a rabbit. He comes to her for help to fix a cape or an engineer's cap, or to make him long ears—whatever he needs to become a special person or animal. Granted, Ruthella doesn't have time for drinking many cups of coffee with anybody, but she is wisely giving her young son the help he needs to explore various areas of his world.

The mother of one of my Cub Scouts called recently to ask for my recipe for modeling clay. She has five youngsters at home and decided to have something new for them to work with. "I've run out of finger-paint material," she explained, "and John wants to make a cage for a baby rabbit he found back in the timber. I want to keep little siblings away from him while he works."

John will get the cage done, too! He will build it and go to the library for stories about rabbits and how to care for them. The next time we have a den meeting he'll bring the bunny to share with us. His horizons are broadening by leaps and bounds.

My most difficult struggle, as I think through this situation, is to let the boys do projects the way they want to. I want to help spread the butterflies, or mix the paint, or measure the flour for the cookies. I want to say, "Be careful, you'll fall," "Don't spill," "Stay inside the lines when you color." But they must find out the answers for themselves and discover their own abilities and talents and grow independent. I should only set the scene, encourage, provide materials if needed, and help only when they ask.

Our children are living in the most exciting era the world has ever known. Their minds need to soar and explore right along with the rockets they see on television and the pictures of a bathysphere in the *National Geographic* magazine. God has put within every child a spark of creativity, a desire to seek and explore and discover. Each one is a unique individual, one who has talents and abilities.

Who knows what paths may open up as a child develops, for being creative can take many forms.

Jeff Runs Away from Home

SURELY IN EVERY child's life comes a time when existence at home becomes intolerable and visions of running away dance tantalizingly before his eyes. I ran away at the tender age of three and promptly wandered into the nearby big public swimming pool area and walked off the deep end into the water. Only the prompt action of an alert lifeguard made it possible for me to sit here and write this column today.

A few years after the swimming pool episode, I wandered again. This time I arrived back home with my arms filled with candy, toys, and the like. My astonished father retraced my steps and discovered I had gone into every store in town and picked up what I wanted and said, "charge it." Since I was the minister's daughter, the store people let me leave with the items. (I still don't know why they didn't realized I shouldn't be in their establishments all alone.)

My father and I took one more trip downtown. We stopped in every store and I returned the articles saying meekly, "I'm sorry." One ice cream cone, which was in no condition to be returned, was paid for with a nickel from my allowance. That really hurt! To my knowledge, that experience ended my running away from home.

Yesterday was a bad day as far as my two youngest children were concerned. Jeff, age five and Craig, age three, started the day with a huge argument. It seemed one of them had a white toy horse. The other one, who had not thought about that small horse until he saw it in his brother's hands, decided that he *had* to have that particular toy. Bedlam ensued. I finally took a hand, literally, to the situation, and when the dust cleared, Jeff looked up indignantly and said, "I'm going to leave this house. Goodbye!"

When I looked into the boys' bedroom a few minutes later, Jeff was taking clothes out of his drawer and putting them into a box. Big brother Bob (nine years old) was still in bed and was watching with great interest.

"Why are you putting in your Sunday shirt?" Bob asked

"So I can go to Sunday school," Jeff's jaw looked firm.

"How will you know when it's time to go to Sunday school?" was Bob's next question.

"When the church bell rings, I'll put on my good shirt and go," Jeff answered.

They discussed at great length where this wanderer would go and where he would put his sleeping bag at night when it got dark. Suddenly, the subject of food came up. "I'll pack you a lunch to take along," I suggested helpfully from my observation post by the door.

Jeff looked up at me in surprise. "Won't you be sad to have me go?" he asked.

"Do you want me to be sad?"

"Yes! I'm mad because you won't ever let me do what I want to do."

"Well, I will miss you very much, but I want you to be happy. Will you come back and eat with us this evening when we have fried chicken for supper?"

For the first time Jeff began to waver. Visions of fried chicken suddenly became more enticing than being able to do anything he pleased.

"I guess I will wait until day after tomorrow, and then I'll run away from home." The crisis was past.

A short time later I looked out the window to see the three boys with their heads close together over the book of Indian handicraft. I had been forgiven.

A Houseful of Men

"NEVER A DULL MOMENT" is a phrase surely written by a mother with a house full of active, busy offspring. It should be tucked in beside "There is no place like home . . . absolutely no place," "This is the happiest time of my life, if I can just live through it!" and the like.

I am the only woman in a house full of men. My dear friend Mary Ann Haas wrote when I gave birth to my third son, "I've always wanted to surround myself with handsome men. Seems to me you've found the formula!"

Living with a house full of such men, big and little, is an engrossing occupation with many sidelines. A mother may begin with warming bottles and changing diapers, but she soon becomes involved in assembling telescopes, explaining Sputnik satellites, finding milkweed pods to take to school, removing splinters, retrieving lost balls, picking up constantly, and drying tears.

The oldest of my masculine brood, junior-grade, is Bob, who turned eight on January 7. I sit and look at the tallness of his frame, the blueness of his eyes, and think of the wisdom accumulated in his few short years. I am amazed that this tall, dark-haired second grader is mine.

He knows all the answers to everything which exists in his world! When the real world becomes too mundane, his imaginary world takes over. Peopled with knights in castles, Peter Pan, Alice and her Wonderland, and pilots on their way to Mars—he goes from one location to another in a blink of an eye. Sometimes he takes his brothers along on these flights of fancy. If they are not cooperative, he drops them without compunction and goes his own merry way.

Reading is Bob's greatest pleasure, whether at school or at home. We couldn't be more pleased. From the encyclopedia to *National Geographic* magazines to Robert Louis Stevenson poems, he is trying to make his own way. Only requested help is accepted from his parents—no volunteer assistance is tolerated. And if you don't know how broadening this is to parents' education you've not had an eight-year-old to stimulate you into detailed learning. Come to think of it, seems like I'm learning more this session of second grade than I gained from my first experience.

Bob has started piano lessons, practicing happily on the old reed organ which graces our living room. Even a little knowledge of instruments will give added pleasure to life, so I'm hoping all the boys may eventually have some musical background.

Jeff is our happy, serious, almost four-year-old. His birthday is on February 25 so I know full well that some of the stubborn individuality of four will soon be showing up. Four, it seems to me, is another two, only on a different level. So I know we are living on a peaceful plateau which will undoubtedly soon vanish in a mountain peak of stormy development. Now he plays contentedly, cutting and pasting and painting strident-hued pictures with his watercolors and brushes. He spends hours and hours and hours listening to his beloved phonograph records.

He talks incessantly, hitting the floor in the morning, going strong, and never stopping until sleep makes it impossible to continue. Looking at books, listening to stories, and singing (everything from "I've Been Working on the Railroad" to "Jesus Loves Me" in a clear sweet voice) are probably his special pleasures at the moment. He has urged us into the old-fashioned habit of singing around the organ for a few minutes each evening, and we are finding it one of the most pleasant times of the day.

Craig's second birthday zoomed by on December 20 and we realized we don't have a baby anymore. He is industriously trying to live up to that statement, too! He is really a big boy who can talk and play and run and get into things all the time.

It has never been in my line of experience to raise a relative to a monkey, but I'm having it now. To date, nothing has stopped Craig's passion for climbing. He crawled out of his high-sided crib when he was nine months old. With complete fearlessness he pushes a chair over to the high chest of drawers and proceeds to add himself to the articles placed on top. Without any concern for his own safety, he clambers over the fence surrounding the yard and the porch railing. Since we live alongside a busy, busy highway this is a *real* matter for concern.

The center of the kitchen stove, the middle of the kitchen sink, and the far reaches of the kitchen cupboards are simply interesting territory for him to explore. The top bunk bed came off its posts and is now on the floor beside the bottom bunk, for fearless Craig discovered he could climb over the end and onto that top bed. Since it doesn't seem to us an appropriate place for a two-year-old to frolic, the high bed came down.

Craig is rapidly losing his baby chubbiness and a little of its charm. Stubborn streaks and "No, no, no!" are coming more to the fore in his disposition. But he is still easily deflected by a tractor, a wagon and a few blocks, or his precious *Copy Kitten* book.

Craig's conversation is rapidly becoming more understandable. It's especially fun to spot the little boy coming through the baby habits. But when he gets tired or is hurt, he reverts to every baby trick seemingly forgotten. With his little sweet head snuggled into the depression in Daddy's shoulder, he cuddles unashamed.

Robert and I understand as never before how quickly these little ones grow up and away. We would not stay them for a minute, but try to enjoy every second of their childhood.

Clean Socks at Summer Camp

TEN-YEAR-OLD BOB has spent the past two weeks at YMCA Camp Foster at Spirit Lake, Iowa. His letters have been surprisingly frequent and newsy. I expected at least two letters, for the grapevine had informed me that once during each week, the boys had to write and place a letter in a box before they were allowed to eat their evening meal. But three letters arrived the first week. Only one came the second, and that was a good sign. He got so deeply involved in the activities of the camp that time to write home was not a priority.

His letters told us a great deal. Mostly: "Boy, I am having fun." "Boy I am sure getting loads of sand in my shoes." "Boy did we have a good breakfast this morning. Pancakes." "Boy, is arcery fun." (I wonder if that is the same as archery?)

And this one: "Boy did we have a night when we camped out. We hiked out to Old Baldy which is a place without grass with trees all around. One boy talked and kicked and tossed all night. I went to sleep about 11:00. At 3:00 I woke up, and there were cows all over the place. Then the tent fell down. Boy did we have fun!"

Mothers of experienced campers told me to lay out the clothes I thought he would need, and then send only half of them. One mother informed me that her son had used one towel for the entire two week's period. Even with all this good advice, I had to be shown! Of the five pairs of socks Bob took with him, he only wore two!

"Why didn't you wear the rest of your socks?" I asked, holding the dirty socks gingerly at arm's length.

"I didn't need them," Bob replied. "I wore one pair one week and you told me to be sure and put clean ones on when Sunday came so I did." At least a change of clothes came about once during the camp session.

Bob's soap came back home still carefully wrapped. His good friend Billy, who had also attended those two weeks, also returned home with his soap carefully encased in paper.

"How come?" was all I could choke out in the way of a question.

"Oh we all used Steve's soap. We wanted to see how many of us could get home without using our own." A really relieved look must have spread across my face. He *had* washed while he was there.

The climax in unpacking came, however, when I pulled a sheet of stationery from the suitcase and glanced at the bottom which said, in a round juvenile hand, "Love and Kisses, Laura." Who in heaven's name was Laura? Why had she written a mushy letter to my ten-year-old? Then I glanced up at the salutation. It began "Dear Henry." That was a relief. I turned to Bob, "Why do you have Henry's love letter in your things?"

"Oh," he shrugged, "Dutch (the cabin counselor) told us to pick up all the papers on the floor, so I just put everything into my suitcase that I found." So that explains the love and kisses which were so carefully carried home from camp.

I have seen a marked change in our young son, which has been both interesting and rewarding. It is our hope that the two weeks at camp gave him needed time away from parental guidance to contribute to his growth toward independence. That time apart has also helped me to appreciate the fact that he is capable of making decisions and can get along without me.

I've matured during these two weeks as well.

Winters Past

THE WINDOWS ON THE porch are all frosted over this morning, reminding me of a time now long gone.

Robert and I lived at Cottonwood Farm in the 1950s, set back from the road and up a long country lane that gave this column its name. The small white house was uninsulated, and when the temperature got down to freezing in the winter, frost formed on the inside of the windows. When this happened, our children loved to take anything metal—thimbles, cookie cutters, and other kitchen utensils and make designs on the windows. They even remember making prints with their warm hands.

I enjoyed that play much less than the boys because the frost formed when chill winds blew tenaciously through the walls of the house and up from under the floor boards.

I remember using the playpen to provide a warm place for the children. I put a blanket on the bottom of the pen, which was about four inches above the floor. Then I hung another blanket on three sides. I placed the pen with the fourth side open toward the oil burning stove in the living room—the only heat source in our house. The children would get inside the playpen to read, color, play with their toys, and stay warm.

Despite all our efforts during the time we lived in that drafty house, our children had croup. What a worry that was. The problem would start with a deep, wheezy, "croupy" cough that was scary in its tendency to cause breathing problems. I learned early on to set a kettle of water on the kitchen stove to heat. When it was steaming, I'd fix a paper cone and either Robert or I would hold the croupy children and help them breath the moist air coming out the top of the cone. When they became available, we bought an electric vaporizer. It sent out warm, moist air for the patient to breathe just as the old tea kettle had done.

When son Bob was about three and one half years old, he had such a severe attack of the croup, we were afraid he was going to choke. Robert called dear Doctor Gottsch in Shenandoah, and the doctor had us bring Bob to the Hand Hospital for observation and care. One of the attending nurses put a packet of crushed ice on the little boy's throat. She also continued the moist steam.

When we moved to the Redd farm south of Sidney, we were in another drafty house. The coal furnace had several registers in the various rooms, so it was warmer than Cottonwood Farm, but it still was drafty, and the croup continued to plague us. Now it was son Jeff who had it most often.

This story has a happy ending. Once we built our house in town and made it snug with enough insulation to keep out any drafts that might be trying to sneak inside, all symptoms of the croup ceased. However, even today, when we have a bad winter storm, I feel concern for every family that is having a problem with heating. Related illnesses can make life very difficult.

I try and remember the good things about those long cold winters—the fun sledding on the hill, sliding on the icy creek, making snowmen and, yes, drawing designs in the frost on the windows.

Be Prepared

Cub Scout Catastrophes

WE LIVED THROUGH the day, just barely, for it was a rough one!

It probably began on the wrong foot because I was tired. The day before had been bright and sunny, and we had driven up to Des Moines for a visit with my mother before she entrained for Arizona and a visit with my sister, Ruth.

But this morning it was raining. Breakfast managed, by the skin of its teeth, to be a tolerable meal. One boy's shoe was missing in spite of the warning the evening before: "Be *sure* and lay out all of your clothes for tomorrow." When we finally found the shoe, the overshoes were nowhere to be found. They were finally unearthed in a corner of the basement.

Just as Jeff shot out the door to the waiting school bus he yelled, "Be sure and lay out the bamboo mat I made at Cub Scouts, I have to take it tonight."

That bamboo mat was important. Jeff, as you know, is the middle boy in our family. He's caught in the long recognized squeeze produced by being younger than the oldest, who can do everything first, and older than the youngest, who can still fall back on baby ways. So we think up all sorts of ideas to help Jeff feel loved, individual, and important. For the last two weeks he has been immersed in the joys of Cub Scouting. He has been trying to do Japanese projects, none of which turned out very well except for the aforementioned mat.

His coolie hat had torn on the way home from a den meeting, and he threw it away. I never even saw it. For some reason, he had not made a Japanese lantern when some of the other boys made theirs. And now, as I turned back into the house after waving goodbye to the boys, I could not remember where he had put the bamboo mat when he rushed in from last Monday's den meeting.

I hunted. I searched. I almost screamed. "Where is that mat?" It was nowhere!

Turning to other duties. I dug out the old dragon pajamas which have served faithfully for several years. I washed, mended, ironed, and sewed buttons on them, added a red sash, and his costume was ready for the pack meeting.

When Jeff arrived home from school, I told him I could not find his mat, so he best make a pretty lantern to take for the display. We got out the paper, watercolors, encyclopedia (to find Japanese designs), and by the time supper was ready he had made a fine paper lantern.

"Let's put a candle inside and see how it looks," brother Craig suggested.

"No way," Jeff responded.

When we arrived at the Cub Scout meeting place, Jeff, in his excitement jumped hurriedly from the car. His Japanese costumes fell, *plop*, in the mud. I could have cried. Jeff looked as if he might. We wiped as much of the mud off as possible, so when it came time for the skit, the other boys put on their outfits. Jeffrey put his on, splatters and all, and soon the pack meeting was over.

Jeff rushed up to his Den Mother. "I thought I was supposed to get my Bobcat pin," he said.

"Oh," she said. "It didn't come."

Jeff recovered from this blow far more rapidly than his mother. He will be looking forward to getting that pin at the next pack meeting. I'm not at all certain I'll be strong enough to make it.

This morning the pajamas and the sash are in the laundry basket. We will make another bamboo mat and hang it importantly on the wall. The lantern stands muddied and proud on top of the piano.

I waved goodbye to the boys as they left on this morning's school bus. I did the supper dishes and the breakfast dishes. I swept the kitchen and made the beds. With a sigh, I realized that after all is said and done, what I really hope is that, despite all the traumas in growing up, Jeff really will turn out all right.

Cub Scout Den Mother

THE CULMINATION OF the years of learning from my father and then helping my Scoutmaster husband and my two older sons with all of their Scouting projects came when youngest son Craig had his eighth birthday. On that December 20, 1963, he received a Cub Scout shirt, a cap, scrapbook, and neckerchief, all beautifully inscribed with the proper emblems. He unwrapped the last gift and burst into sobs.

"I've got all this scout stuff and no den for me to join," Craig stammered through his tears.

He spoke the truth. Neither of the active dens in Sidney had room for one more boy. The handwriting on the wall was crystal clear, but I held out a little longer. Then the Cub Master came to see if I would lead a den.

"Maybe in June if you can't find anyone else," I suggested, hoping another mother would surface before that time.

June, unfortunately, was a long way off. Craig's Cub Scout shirt hung limp in the closet as Jeff went off to his den and Bob went off to his troop and Robert went off to his Scout meetings. Craig's face grew long and sad.

Besides coping with Craig's pleading, here came more boys without a den. They urged and their parents telephoned and the sad faces increased in number and intensity. Life just wasn't worth living at all for those of us left out of all the excitement.

Well, I can stand just so much, so I finally decided that I would have to find the time to work with a Cub Scout den.

Quicker than you can say, "Do your best," I had ten boys coming to the basement of our house and Den 2 of Pack 77, Sidney, Iowa, was born.

The first meeting was wonderful. The boys were quiet, seemingly awed by the momentous occasion. We painted bears and lions and wolves on brown paper grocery sacks, then each boy printed his name on his own and slipped it over the back of his chair. (This was a fun project but it also gave me a clue as to the right name for which boy and provided some control over the seating arrangements).

We progressed through charts of birds, made nesting materials, hummingbird feeders, and plaster casts of animal footprints. We planted seeds. We made kites and had a kite-flying derby.

The boys built bird houses as a father-son project. We pledged allegiance to the flag, gave the Scout promise, formed a living circle, played wild and noisy games, and yelled the Cub yell.

I learned which of the boys were determined workers and which were the let's-fool-around types. I had one who liked to make weird faces and one who jumped around a lot.

During the Mexican project we memorized some Spanish words, learned some traditions and games (including a fun piñata), and discovered that tacos need to be cooked before being eaten. When the weather was warm we played out-of-doors and became adept at making s'mores and roasting hot dogs over a small camp fire in our yard.

Not long ago I was sitting in the dentist's waiting room in Shenandoah, Iowa. A tall, good looking gentleman came in, looked at me for a second and then smiled. He greeted me warmly. "I know you. You are my Den Mother. I have never forgotten the things we did and how much being a Cub Scout meant to me. I'm Frank Hammons." And we sat and talked of his successful business and his fine family. When I was called back into the dentist's patient room, Frank said, "Thanks, Cub Mother."

If I had not had the tears and the pressure of my youngest son and the needs of other boys in our town, I would not have experienced the whole, wonderful, vigorous, exciting world of Cub Scouting. Once I became a Den Mother, I was a vital part of the Scout system. I wouldn't have missed that for anything.

Bob Becomes a Scout

IT WAS WITH A great feeling of pride that I watched the two Scout men in my family go out the door last week. Robert has been Scoutmaster here in Sidney for some time. Every Monday he put on his Scoutmaster shirt, gathered his paraphernalia together for the meeting, and left. Young Bob watched all of this preparation with longing eyes. Just wait, though, he would think, some day I will be old enough to go too.

As it always does, time passed, and in January 1961, Bob reached his goal. He became eleven years old! Not only had he achieved the age needed to become a Scout, but he had also received a number of fine Christmas gifts of needed Scouting gear.

The shirt and neckerchief are most important (no tie slides, please —he'd make his own). The knife and the canteen set were, however, interesting and useable. Since money also came for his birthday, he is going to buy his own Scout cap. He decided to use part of the gift money to pay for his Scouting dues, which makes him personally responsible for his new status.

So last Monday, when his father began to pick up Scout books, tree branches, and a saw for demonstrations, plus some game ideas for the troop meeting, Bob was right there beside him. He offered suggestions, he helped gather together what was needed, and then he combed his hair carefully with the "Official Boy Scout comb." He looked at himself with a critical eye in the "Official Boy Scout mirror" to be sure his neckerchief was tied correctly. Then Bob went around mumbling such phrases as: "A Scout is kind," "A Scout is reverent," "A Scout is helpful!"

"Aha," I interrupted. "Now I'll have a *real willing* helper around this house at last!"

"Oh, no! That just means I help old ladies across the street!" Bob grinned.

"I'll be the old lady before long if I don't get some good assistance right here at home."

But we both know he has always been good help and would continue to be. (It is the *cheerful* part which will be put to the test when it is time to empty the garbage, keep track of his younger brothers, and help with the dishes.)

It seemed like a long evening before the two Scouts finally returned from their meeting. Bob burst through the front door beaming. "I made it!" he shouted as he flung himself at me in a big bear hug.

"You're going to be a good Scout." I hugged back.

"I'm sure glad Dad is the Scoutmaster."

"You'll have to work harder than anyone else in the troop. Your father won't let you get away with anything," I said.

"Yes, I know that, but I'll learn more, too!"

So, it looks as if father and son Scouts are getting off to a good start together.

One reason I feel such a glow of satisfaction over this situation goes clear back to my childhood. My own father was a Scoutmaster and guided many boys through the years. I wish my father could have lived to know and enjoy his grandsons. But that was not be.

That evening, as my eldest son walked out the door with his father to start on this new adventure, I said a thankful prayer that Robert had a son of his own in his troop, happy with the knowledge that he has years and years of adventure with all three sons ahead of him.

Freeze Outs

"WHAT A GREAT DAY for a Boy Scout Freeze Out," Bill Penn said to Robert one day when the temperature hovered near zero, and snow covered the ground.

"It sure would be," Robert answered. "But I don't know if the kids today would enjoy it. I don't see anyone sliding on Oldsmobile Hill or coasting out in the North Street pasture like we used to."

As Robert walked the five blocks home from Penn's drug store, he thought of all the Freeze Outs he enjoyed as Scoutmaster for Troop 77 of Sidney. No doubt, as he went back to his pharmaceutical efforts, Bill Penn remembered them as well.

Each year, as winter grew long and the Scouts grew restless, Robert would decree it was time to pack their warmest gear and head for the bluffs, Draper's timber (this was before the trees were cut down and the hills planted to corn) or Manti Park for an overnighter. Sometimes the troop would go to one of the Scout District Freeze Outs, where they would shiver around a campfire with Scouts from other troops.

If the weather was warm during such an outing, it was considered a near catastrophe. A Freeze Out was *supposed* to be cold. It was *supposed* to test the youngest Tenderfoot's mettle. If the water didn't turn to ice in the canteens, the outing was not considered a true test of their stamina.

Memorable winter camps for the Sidney boys included one bitterly cold trip when one of the Scouts stood too close to the fire as he warmed his backside and the heat melted holes in his insulated boots. Another boy decided it was too cold to take his boots off when it was time to crawl into his sleeping bag, so in he went, snowy boots and all, and slept in them. All night.

Another time, Troop 77 hiked out in the Loess Hills west of Sidney. It was New Year's Eve day, and a damp, freezing rain started falling soon after they put up their tents.

Robert's nephew, Mike Barnard, was one of the Scouts, so his mother Ruthella (Robert's sister) and I drove out late in the afternoon to deliver the sleeping equipment and big kettles of homemade stew.

The weather was miserable—worse than a snow or below-zero temperature—for the dampness permeated everything and every body. "Such a trip did make the kids appreciate warm houses and comfortable beds," Robert remembered afterwards.

And what did the boys learn from these experiences? How to survive in the cold, how to care for frostbite (do not rub or massage—cover the frozen fingers or toes or ears with warm hands), how to prevent hypothermia, that killer which can happen to anyone who is not dressed warm enough for the air around him. Most of all, they remembered the wise words in the *Boy Scout Handbook*: "If bad weather catches you in the back country, put up your tent, and crawl into your sleeping bag. Eat plenty of food and drink lots of fluid."

Winter provides many an interesting activity in the out-of-doors. Map and compass, orienteering, tracking, snowshoeing, cross-country skiing, building igloos, telling stories around the campfire, and learning about individual limitations, strengths, and endurances.

I hope that youngsters still go out and slide on hills, on snowy city streets, and in country pastures, that they go on freeze outs, and that mothers (or the Scouts themselves) cook up stews for a hearty meal. Winter in Iowa can be wonderful.

Visiting Scouts

IT ALL BEGAN WHEN Robert came home one noon from his work at the ASCS office in Sidney, Iowa, and asked me to guess who was coming for dinner. I came up with the names of many people we have known through the years. He shook his head at each suggestion. Not until lunch was on the table and I had seated myself to look at him curiously did Robert answer my obvious question. "Who is coming? Tell me for goodness sake!"

"Forty Boy Scouts from Japan," came back Robert's unexpected answer.

"Forty Scouts—" I sputtered into silence. Then a sudden thought struck me, "Not tonight?"

"Don't panic. Not tonight," Robert laughed. "You'll have plenty of time to prepare. Besides, the main part of the meal will be picked up in Omaha when the boys get in on their plane. All we really need to provide is something for them to drink with their dinner."

Gradually, then, Robert told me the exciting news. Some thirty-three young Scouts and seven adult leaders from Shizuoka City, Japan, were coming to spend three weeks in the Omaha area. (Omaha is the American sister city of Shizuoka City, Japan.) Since the day the boys were to arrive coincided with the final evening performance of the Sidney Rodeo, the hosts in Omaha thought it would make an excellent place for these Japanese visitors to start their exploration of the United States. This prompted a call to the Sidney Scoutmaster (one Robert Birkby) and his subsequent invitation for the boys to eat their first meal in this country in our backyard!

As the time drew near, we borrowed picnic tables from neighbors, set them out on the lawn near the big mulberry tree, and covered them with bright cloths. Robert and I sliced garden-ripe tomatoes, brought up lime pickles from the basement and spooned them into bowls, and made up big pitchers of iced tea and fruit punch and a large pot of coffee for the adults.

Unfortunately, many of the Sidney Scouts and their families were involved in rodeo activity, and the Japanese Scouts had such a short time in Sidney that it was impossible to get the two groups together during this meal. Our own three sons were off working at the National Scout Ranch in Philmont, New Mexico, so they were not home to share in the experience either.

The day of the visit was beautiful, clear, and sunny. The drive by bus from Omaha to Sidney was along the scenic Loess Hills and the Missouri River area of western Iowa. The Japanese guests alighted from the bus at the front of our house with smiles on their lips and gracious compliments: "So nice." "Beautiful country." "Fine." "Hello."

Once everyone was seated at the tables, each Scout opened a cardboard package containing his dinner. The menu was as American as apple pie (without the pie!): fried chicken; French-fried potatoes; corn-on-the-cob impaled on a sucker-type stick for easier eating, drenched in butter, and wrapped in a tight plastic bag; cabbage slaw; a hot roll; and honey. With a few pantomimed instructions, the boys were soon enthusiastically eating the food with their fingers with the exception of the salad and tomatoes.

How, we wondered, does one ask what people would like to drink when they do not speak English? One doesn't! We just began pouring and saying as we did, "tea" or "punch" or "juice" or "coffee." Those boys quickly picked up the words, and when it came time to refill their cups, they knew exactly what they wanted and spoke clearly!

Hurrying to get to the rodeo performance in time, we could not linger long in the cool shade of the mulberry tree in the backyard of our house after everyone finished eating. Since our home is not far from the rodeo grounds, we all walked. It was quite a group that finally arrived at the stands: the forty visitors, several adult leaders, including some from Omaha, several of our Sidney Scouts, Robert, and finally, me.

It is difficult to say exactly how much of the rodeo performance the guests could comprehend for they could not understand the announcer's comments, but the fact that they enjoyed the evening was beyond question. The color, excitement, music, acts, and personalities were all appreciated. They understood easily that Roger Miller was a television star. Monte Montana was identified as a movie cowboy. The lively action, the rugged performers, the funny clowns, and the trained buffalo all held the attention of the visitors.

The following week, the Japanese contingent were encamped at the Little Sioux Ranch south of Sioux City. This first camp at the new facility for the Mid-America Council was called "Amikaro" which means "a gathering of friends." Two Japanese boys camped, cooked, ate, slept, and participated in the projects of each troop, which included Scouts from Iowa and Nebraska.

Our Sidney boys, who participated in the event, would gladly have brought their two guests home and kept them here; they liked them that well! Robert attended as one of the leaders and reported the week a valuable experience for everyone.

Several interested people from Sidney, including me, were able to drive up to the Little Sioux Camp to attend guest night near the end of the Amikaro week. The camp was dedicated at an impressive ceremony followed by a barbecue dinner for all the Scouts and the guests. The evening concluded with a great campfire lighted by a representative Scout from the United States and one from Japan. We sang songs together, watched the Japanese boys present graceful native dances, and shared a brilliant display of fireworks to conclude a truly fine "gathering of friends."

When the camp was over, our boys came home to Sidney, and the Shizuoka Scouts left for a few days' visit in Omaha. Before returning to Japan, they went west with stops at the Grand Canyon and Las Vegas, Nevada.

When Robert arrived home from Little Sioux, he brought two lovely Japanese prints as gifts from our guests. These have been added, now, to the lovely items our son Craig brought home from his visit a year ago to Shizuoka City when he attended the World Scout

Jamboree in their country. However, the gift I treasure most is a tape recording of a song which the Japanese Scouts sang to us just before they left on the evening they visited our home.

Following the rodeo, the boys made a brief stop at the house for a drink of water and bathroom break before getting back on their bus. I stepped outside to tell them goodbye and found them lined up in straight rows on the grass. The stars were bright and clear above their heads and the flickering glow of our yard light illuminated their youthful faces. They began singing a song in their native language.

This is the song one of the leaders gave to Robert on tape just before he left Amikaro. Now I have the music, the words, and the memory of that wonderful evening. The leader wrote the words on a card for Robert and me, plus their English translation:

> Beautiful starlight, stars in the dark of the sky.
> A gathering of friends and cheerful singing.
> We thank you today; we are happy.
>
> I too, as I remember our time together, am happy.

Pity Mrs. Noah

Three-year-old Bob and his new puppy Silver, January 1954.

Spiders, Skunks, and Salamanders

AS THE YEARS GO BY, my sympathy and understanding for Mrs. Noah increases enormously. Just imagine trying to keep house in an ark filled with animals. So many and such a variety in a comparatively small space without yard or pasture would tax the patience of a saint. The few unusual specimens of wildlife that have made their way into this household have been small indeed compared to Mrs. Noah's situation. Nevertheless, I've found my patience strained on a number of occasions.

The fact that Robert was a Boy Scout executive when we were married catapulted me immediately into the broad world of the out-of-doors. Driving along a beautiful mountain road in Arkansas on our Ozark honeymoon, Robert suddenly slammed on the brakes. He reached in the backseat for a milk carton left from our picnic lunch and leaped from the car. After scooping something up from the side of the road, he turned proudly and presented me with my first gift from the wilds—a tarantula spider.

Robert assured me that the wild, hairy, long-legged thing was not poisonous, but it looked ferocious so I asked him please to shut it tightly into the trunk of the car before we continued our drive.

This should have warned me of things to come. (I wonder what kind of warning Mrs. Noah had.) On a later excursion to the Ozarks, Robert caught another tarantula and proudly carried it home to our three sons. They, equally proud, carried it off to school. I stayed away from school for a time after this educational contribution. It seemed wise.

"Hairy George," as the spider became known, did not live long in captivity, but we learned much about the creature and its habits during his brief stay in a large glass jar.

Another odd pet that was brought in from the field one day was a half-grown bull snake, which the boys promptly christened Blackie. (Mrs. Noah had boys. Did they name all the animals in the ark?)

Now bull snakes are much prized by farmers—alive, not dead. They are excellent helpers in keeping rats and mice under control. They do grow large and are comparatively homely, but on most farms, strict orders go out to leave them alone.

It took a sturdy cage to keep Blackie confined, and he obviously resented every minute of captivity. After observing him for several days, and reading all the stories we could find about snakes, friendly and unfriendly, Robert took him back to the field to go his helpful way. I was the only one honestly glad to see him go.

Next came Little Fellow. He was a cute golden hamster, a great deal like a chipmunk, tucking seeds into pouches in his cheeks until he could hardly wobble over to hide his treasure under the soft bedding in his cage. He cleaned himself like a kitten, licking a tiny paw and then rubbing his face and ear meticulously. He sat up on his hind legs like a squirrel to beg or nibble on a sunflower seed.

Just when I thought life was going to settle down to the common run of dogs and kittens and hamsters, Craig came up with the request for a pet skunk.

"A skunk?" I almost shouted. "Wherever did you get the idea you wanted a skunk?"

"I don't remember when I first thought of it," Craig turned a pleading look my way. "But they do make nice pets, a lot like a cat. If I can locate one may I have it?"

Finding a skunk seemed so far from possibility, I promptly dismissed it from my mind. I should have known Craig would not forget. A local farmer found a baby skunk and before I could yell "Help" we had a de-scented, rabies-treated, cute little black and white skunk named "Sniffles" living in our basement.

Craig and his dad spent several happy evenings building a sleeping cage for this new pet. Sniffles likes it just fine. He does like to get out and roam around the basement. So far I've refused to allow him upstairs unless Craig has him firmly on a leash. The books assure me that skunks can be trained, but since Sniffles can't read and I don't have the time or patience to cope, he'll just have to settle for the basement and Craig can train him there.

Craig and Sniffles are quite a pair outdoors. Sniffles ambles along or gallops or stops and looks around for insects. Our big black collie "Wheels" takes a very dim view of this creature. The skunk, who is small enough to make one mouthful for the dog, stamps his feet and plumes out his tail. The dog whiffles her nose a bit and retreats with cautious disgust around the corner of the house.

Pets teach parents and children both. Ours have brought us close to nature. By both observation and study, we have learned to appreciate even the most homely. Caring for pets helps youngsters grow in taking responsibility. It helps mothers develop more patience and understanding. We have all gained more reverence for God's creatures. I wonder if that is what held Mrs. Noah steady through that long confining voyage?

A Company Keeper Called Silver

ALTHOUGH HIS SISTER could never be replaced, we provided Bob with a new dog to help with his loneliness. In September of 1953, a sad little three-year-old boy went to find a pet. His closest friend, playmate, and sister Dulcie Jean had died just three months earlier.

When we stood by the large litter of puppies waiting for his choice, the wait was short. Bob hesitated only a second and then scooped up a wiggly, roly-poly, all-white puppy with sharp-looking blue eyes.

"I want this puppy. He has a nice face."

The puppy Bob chose not only had a nice face but a perfect disposition for a boy's dog. We named him Silver, after the Lone Ranger's big white horse. Silver was a good companion to all of us, following Robert out to the field, prancing underfoot when I went out to hang up the clothes, and romping with all of us with puppy fierceness.

In the spring our second son, Jeff, was added to Silver's responsibilities, and then two years later, a third, Craig. By this time the dog was deep-chested with a regal head. Enough of his mother's collie blood came through to make him a really majestic-looking animal.

Silver's patience was tremendous. The amount of running, chasing, hiking, roaming, and noise-making of three boys can be overwhelming, but Silver took it all in stride. He was a fine watchdog, not because of any fierce qualities, but because his large size intimidated anyone who came near.

He had three serious incidents. First, his foot was cut badly by a mower. Second, he was struck by a car when we moved to the house by a busy highway. It caught him across the nose, making it forever crooked but giving Silver a fear of the pavement which may well have saved his life at a future date. Then, last fall, he decided he was a dog, and spent three days wandering miles to the east of home base, coming back bedraggled and hungry and wiser, for he did not venture out again.

Silver had never been sick, as far as we knew, for even a minute. But one day in the winter of 1959 Silver began refusing food, drooping, and looking really ill. The veterinary doctor made several trips out and gave him medication. We spoon-fed the dog egg with milk and sugar. He did not seem to suffer, but day by day, he grew weaker on a pallet in the basement.

Late in the week Robert took some milk down for him, but Silver would not eat. He did drink a bit of cool water, managed to flip the end of his tail in a final greeting, laid his big white head with its slightly crooked nose down on the blanket, and died.

We did not tell the boys the next morning, for it was a big rush to get them off to school, and there was no time to talk. All day I dreaded the moment when I would have to give them the news.

Bob and Jeff piled off the school bus in fine high spirits, not missing Silver's greeting bark for they knew he had been sick. At 4:30 I knew the time had come, for any delay would run too close to supper and bedtime.

Bob burst into hard bitter tears, then went off to tell Jeff. Jeff was inconsolable. His grief was complete, all consuming, and rebellious. When his sobs at last subsided, he lifted his head from my shoulder, looked at Bob for reassurance, and Bob gave it to him in a very grownup manner. I was proud of my nine-year-old.

The boys wanted to know if Daddy had buried Silver, I told them yes, down by the creek he loved so well, under a big tree. The boys immediately wanted to go see, and I said fine. Craig, without tears, with limited comprehension at age four, was ready to go along and be a part of whatever was taking place.

Soon the boys were back and in deep discussion in their room. I glanced in to see three heads close together over a board on which Bob was printing carefully in his green enamel model paint "SILVER 1953–1959." With a hammer, nail, the board, and the new Bible Bob just received from Sunday school last week, the boys once more trudged back across the road. Tears came to my eyes as I watched them. These were the three humans Silver loved most. I knew the healing of their tears had come, and the drama and interest in this new situation had taken hold of their imagination.

A short time later Jeff bounded into the kitchen. "The ceremony is over," he announced.

"What did you do for your service?" I asked Bob as he and Craig followed Jeff into the house.

"I read the 23rd Psalm, the 100th Psalm, and then just leafed through the Bible and read lots of verses. Then we said a prayer and that was all."

I am certain a God, who made good dogs for little boys' companions, understands that such a service is a genuine expression of love.

Our yard now seems silent and empty. No longer do I feel confident in sending Craig out to play alone since he has no guarding companion. Life is not as secure without our watchdog.

Silver was exactly the right dog for the time we needed him most. Someday we will get another dog, but we will always remember Silver, who was a loyal friend and companion who dedicated his whole life to the five humans he loved so completely.

The Snake Trap

SEVEN-YEAR-OLD JEFF and five-year-old Craig have finally discovered that two heads are better than one. It has taken them five years to come to this conclusion. For the first year of Craig's life, Jeff just enjoyed him as if he were a toy. He was "our" brother. The fun of sitting and listening to me read Jeff a story as I fed Craig made having a baby brother an advantage. Craig was a happy, easygoing, little one, which simplified the situation tremendously.

But the day came when Craig stood up on his chubby legs, began to roam the house, and look around. What he saw that interested him most were Jeff's possessions. For the next few years, the rivalry between the two brothers waxed and waned, blew wild and stormy. As I glanced at the embattled brothers I would think of statements my friends have expressed, saying that children who are close together in age are pals, friends, and far easier to manage than those separated by years.

Gradually, the statements of my friends began to make more sense. Jeff and Craig are beginning to find more in common. They play side by side for longer periods of time without a squabble and they are discovering the advantages of two minds plotting together.

Now I am faced with a new predicament. I hear the boys whispering excitedly in the far corner of the playroom. What are they planning? Is it desirable? Is it safe? Is it *messy*? I see them going off across the grass toward the chicken house gathering sticks and rocks as they go. Is it ammunition they are collecting? Are they planning a campfire? Had I better check their pockets? They have never gotten into matches, but that is no reason to think they *never* will.

At least when they did battle, I could hear them and know where they were.

Last Sunday afternoon Craig and Jeff were playing contentedly in the basement when I heard a loud crashing noise. I called down the stairs, "What's falling?"

"Our rattlesnake trap," Jeff yelled back.

"Your *what*?"

"We got some boxes off the shelf and are making a rattlesnake cage. They fell down."

Knowing Jeff as I do, if a real, honest-to-goodness rattlesnake ever so much as looked at him, he'd be out of sight in no time flat. Also, I've lived almost my entire life in Iowa and have never once seen a poisonous reptile.

Just then Jeff came upstairs and explained to me their technique for catching the snake. "After we get the box made, we'll catch a mouse. We'll put the mouse in the box and sit on the box and hold up the lid. When the snake goes in the box to get the mouse we'll shut the lid."

After hearing this method of capture, I relaxed my mental picture of five- and seven-year-old wild animal hunters.

Craig and Jeff spent several happy hours on their snake cage and then went outdoors to the small timber and creek area south of the house. Late in the day, however, Jeff came inside and asked for a jar.

"Why do you want a jar?" I asked cautiously.

"We didn't find a rattlesnake but I did find this brown bug, so I need a jar to keep it in."

The hunt had been a success.

Sammy the Salamander

IF IT ISN'T ONE THING, it's another, and now it is a salamander. If the boys hadn't insisted on going hiking last Sunday we would never have become involved with this lowly, dragon-like creature. We went west of our house on a hike along the country road which goes up and down the hills. When the road turned, we continued straight into the bluffs and timber, across creeks, up banks softened by the recent rains, over fences, and along cow paths.

The line of marchers ahead of me suddenly stopped. Since I am usually lagging behind, it takes several seconds at best for me to find out whatever attracts everyone's attention enough to stop the forward movement. When I moved closer, I could see that in the center of our path was a hole. Sticking his head out of the hole, in complete amazement at the humans who had suddenly entered his world, was a small, translucent green salamander.

Quicker than you could say, "Be prepared," the boys went into action. Bob got a forked stick. Robert sharpened the ends. Jeff and Craig stood poised on each side of the earthen passageway to keep the animal from escaping. With a quick motion, Bob brought the stick in a downward motion and onto the neck of the still motionless creature. He was *ours*!

Once we arrived back home, I brought out a big white enamel dishpan and put it on the back porch. The boys added rocks, foliage, and water so "Sammy" could have a proper home. They have been feeding him bites of hamburger waved enticingly on the end of a broom straw (salamanders routinely eat live insects which explains the waving).

One day Sammy attended Bible school, which caused consternation among the teachers and excitement among the children. On another afternoon Sammy discovered he could slither over the edge of the dishpan. We found him going 'round and 'round the brim of Robert's big straw hat that had been left in one corner of the porch. Why he chose the straw hat, we do not know, not being salamanders.

One evening Craig carried Sammy, dishpan and all, into his bedroom. It seemed all right to me to let the pet sleep close to one of his special people. In the night I heard Craig talking. Sammy had gotten out of his quarters and had climbed up the sheet and onto Craig's bed. "I think he was lonesome," Craig explained when I went into his room to see what was happening.

It took a bit of doing to persuade Craig that sleeping with a salamander might not be good for the little lizard. I put Sammy back into his pan and returned him to the back porch, carefully hooking the screen and shutting the door into the kitchen in the event that Sammy got lonesome again and would be tempted to try and get back into Craig's room.

The children are finding him a fascinating pet, and even I am growing accustomed to his homely appearance.

Friends in Our Yard

IT IS SURPRISING how many friends we have in our yard— everything from grasshoppers and crickets to a cute yellow kitten who wandered over from the neighbors.

Recently nine-year-old Craig called me to come see a new inhabitant of our green kingdom. A cicada was clinging tightly to the rough bark of the mulberry tree and undertaking the fascinating process of shedding its old shell. We watched, entranced, for a long period of time, as the delicate insect struggled and pushed its way out of the old encasement.

"Don't touch him until he's good and dry and strong," Craig cautioned. He might catch that same cicada later in the week to keep for his insect collection, but at this moment it was a creature to be protected and admired simply for its courage and tenacity, a miracle of nature.

One day this summer, a camel cricket appeared between the house and the mailbox, headed west, Jeff said. We thought this humpbacked insect was native to western states so decided it had ridden in on my sister Ruth's car when she drove up from Arizona.

Later a friend informed us that this insect is the same as the cave crickets that live in the dark caves in many of our states. I am not expert enough to know if they are the same, but Jeff still insists that this particular cricket was headed back to Arizona when he caught him!

Birds have been cheerful companions in our yard this summer: a yellow-billed mocking bird, several bluebirds in the birdhouses among the apple trees, robins nesting unafraid in the low branches of the mulberry tree (where the boys watched the eggs and baby robins through two complete cycles), and a whole colony of purple martins.

Did you know purple martins are very fond of flying bugs? When they go swooping and gliding in their deep, graceful dives they are not just entertaining bird watchers, they are catching flying insects (mosquitoes especially, bless them). Our purple martin house provides space for fourteen families. It now shelters twelve martins, and two are sets of sparrow parents. "Integrated housing," Robert explains.

We have a few residents in our yard who are not particularly welcome, just tolerated. Wasp and killer bees and bumblebees are not in any great quantity, but they are around. In fact, at this very moment, I am looking out the window at the lush foliage and delicate trumpets of the heavenly blue morning glories that frame the front of the house. Flying deep into one of the blue horns is a huge bumblebee. Craig's instinct for a dangerous insect has held steady this summer, and he has been careful of these stinging creatures when he goes outside, net in hand, to capture new insects, so the bumblebees have not bothered us.

Our yard is well populated with boys, too, and on occasion, a girl or two wanders by. At the moment, my sons are digging a "secret" tunnel under the shack Craig built while his brothers are away attending summer camp. When he announced his plans, it seemed like an innocent enough project, but soon cousin Mike arrived with shovel in hand, and neighborhood children came over to see what was going on and stayed to dig.

It is one thing to have a single boy dig away at a hole, but add several with shovels and wagons and visions of a Grand-Canyon-like abyss arise.

Robert, fortunately, is a patient, long-suffering father. He knows boys well and understands that they need a place in which to build shanties and dig holes. *But*, he also knows when it is time to call a halt and keep activity from getting out of hand.

"Halt," he yelled. And despite tears and pleadings, he stood adamant. So halt they did. The tunnel is now as deep and as long as it is going to be.

So, as you can see, our yard is a busy and fascinating place, one which continues to provide new and interesting experiences. In fact, a skittery hummingbird has just come up to the morning glory next to my window to get a late lunch. If you'll excuse me, I will stop my typing and take the time to get acquainted with one more friend who lives in our yard.

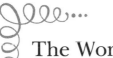

The World of Ants

RECENTLY, OUR BOYS and some of the neighbor children were playing outside. They were all young enough that a period of intense quiet meant that I should investigate. Realizing that such a moment had come, I looked outside to see a cluster of heads over one spot in the yard.

As I drew near the group, son Jeff signaled for me to be very quiet. I soon realized that the center of all the children's attention was a large ant hill. The busy members of this insect community were rushing back and forth carrying out their various duties. The boys watched, commenting in whispers on the purpose of this action and that movement. Completely ignored, I tiptoed softly back to the house. In a few moments, Craig came into the house long enough to get some of our books on insects.

It was suppertime before interest waned and the children went off to their various homes. During our evening meal Jeff and Craig told their father and me of the wonders of life among the ants. No one had planned their afternoon. No teacher had assigned the research or the final report. Out of natural curiosity of lively minds, the boys watched, searched for answers, and shared their findings. It was a rewarding day for us all.

In the years that Robert had taken his sons (and other people's sons in Boy Scout projects) on campouts and to Scout camp, he had stressed this idea of looking and listening and finding the answers to nature. On a recent Scout hike, he found a small animal skeleton beside the trail. Stopping, he asked the boys to try to reconstruct what might have happened to the tiny animal. Before the troop moved on, they had thought through the cycle of nature and survival: a small rabbit ate plants and in turn provided food for a predator, probably a hawk. His lessons have carried over into the everyday lives of our sons, even taking them into the exciting world of ants.

Our Own Husky

SPREAD OUT ON THE table are several booklets with such fascinating titles as *Dog Sleds and Harness Styles*, *Building a Training Cart*, and *Packing Dogs*. They are being carefully read and digested.

The object of all this intensive research could care less. He is curled up with his nose warmly tucked into his tail, snugly asleep in his doghouse. This is the large red doghouse which once belonged to our big black collie, Wheels. I heard recently of a family that antiqued their doghouse in preparation for a new puppy. Well, we didn't have to bother with ours. It started out Colonial Red, but it has weathered into a lovely antique shade of old barn.

Our Alaskan husky was born October 16, 1965, in Neligh, Nebraska. He arrived in Sidney just in time for Robert's birthday on November 24, so he really belongs to Robert. After long deliberation with the family, Robert finally named him Attu. It is the name of an island in the Aleutian chain, and we do hope the word has a meaning which is fitting for an Alaskan dog.

Attu is buff and white. His markings are like those seen in most pictures of Eskimo dogs; he has a white nose and then his ears and markings down toward each eye are buff. He has a white ruff around his neck, and his back is the same light tan color as his ears. His paws are white. Even for such a young dog, he keeps himself surprisingly clean, one of the qualities for which huskies are noted.

The most striking aspects of Attu's appearance are his eyes. He has the deep blue eyes that are found among some northern dogs. The blue eyes are startling enough in the puppy's white face, but then, to add glamour, they are edged with black, just as if someone had taken an eyeliner and intentionally gone around the edge of each eye. He is a quick, alert, and intelligent puppy. I can see why these dogs are used as helpers in the far north, for they surely can be trained in many ways.

Jeff and Craig can hardly wait until Attu is old enough to carry a backpack or be taught to pull a small training cart or sled. Along about April or May they hope he will be old enough and big enough to start off at least with a light backpack and go across the bluffs on a hike. Since the books we've been reading suggest waiting for serious training until six or seven months of age, this sounds like a good time schedule for Attu.

This cute teddy bear of a puppy has already provided us with much pleasure and some laughs. The other afternoon, I was working in the basement when I heard a sharp, pained cry. I rushed upstairs and there was Attu back in the farthest corner of the patio making a great commotion. He was not cowering, far from it. He was standing firm and as tall as his puppy legs would hold him. Coming across the yard was the biggest dog in town and he must have looked like a monster to Attu.

Vike is a Great Dane who belongs to Roger Eitzmann, the wrestling and football coach of our Sidney High School. Vike had simply wandered across a few backyards and come to call.

Telling Vike to go home, I picked up Attu and informed him all was well. Attu grasped my arm with his sturdy front paws, licked my hand, and the crisis was over.

Of course, one crisis can quickly follow another. The very next day I heard another howling cry of concern. Attu was firmly chained in the backyard, and my first thought was that he might have become entangled. When I reached the yard I could only stand and laugh. Delicately, gently tiptoeing across the frozen stalks of grass were five tiny Persian kittens. They were so small, it surely must have been their first outing away from their mother. From the fuss Attu was making you would have thought five Great Danes were stalking across the yard. The kittens paid no attention to the ferocious-sounding puppy until they were almost within reach of his paws when the lead kitten spat and lifted up a paw with teeny claws extended. This so startled

Attu that he sat back on his haunches, quit howling, and just looked at the audacious creature.

A bit later, that same kitten was tucked right under Attu's chin and he was busily licking the fuzzy fur with a loving tongue. "See," Attu seemed to say as he looked up at me with an almost grin, "I've got a pet too."

As I look at our fast-growing puppy I realize an Alaskan husky is a lot of dog. Our Attu certainly is one prime example. We are trying to do a good job training him as a helpful, happy pet.

The Bees of Honey Hill

IF YOU VISITED in our home, it would not take long for you to discover that the Birkby family has a thing about bees and honey. Take some of the knickknacks around the house, for example. A silver bank shaped like a beehive stands on the dining room hutch. A short white rope with a hive-shaped base hangs on the frame of the living room door. Fastened to this interesting conversation piece are several artificial bees and cheerful white daisies.

A pottery hive stands in the kitchen. Craig made this one about five years ago in ceramics class at school. Lovingly coiled and topped with a dainty molded bee, it is glazed yellow and fired to a firm finish. All these years that hive has held the supply of honey we use on the table.

Anyone who had known my husband Robert long would have guessed that sooner or later he would get into the beekeeping business. When he was a small boy, he had a neighbor who raised bees. Fascinated by the useful insects, he watched and learned. Later as a Scout leader he continued to develop his knowledge. A friend in Farragut, Iowa, Ben Hall, was an experienced beekeeper and began counseling the Scouts, even loaning exhibition frames full of bees to Robert's troop for demonstration purposes at Scout circuses and fairs. A neighbor gave Robert an empty hive, which the Scouts also used for their various events.

One June evening Robert received a phone call from his Aunt Mildred Reed, who lives in our hometown of Sidney. She told him that a large swarm of bees was fastened to one of her small fruit trees. What should she do? Robert told his aunt to do nothing, he would be right over.

With son Craig as a willing helper, Robert carted his empty hive across town. The heavy, elongated cluster of bees was hanging quietly from a low branch. Robert placed the empty hive on the ground under the bees, put newspapers around the entrance to form a ramp, and gently shook the branch so many of the bees dropped onto the newspapers. He brushed the bees into the hive with a leafy twig, being careful to see that the queen bee went inside as well.

In the mysterious way bees communicate, the bees in the hive sent out a message to the swarm above that they had found a fine, spacious home and the queen was in residence. The remaining bees began to move in. By the following morning, all the bees were in the hive and Robert brought it back to a new location by his apple trees. Thus began the Honey Hill bee colony, and the origin of the name for our small acreage.

Our fascination and appreciation of bees continues. On a warm spring day, I can stand at the kitchen window and watch our busy bees as they make a "beeline" from the hives to the birdbath which provides them with water. If we go outside we can spot other beelines as the workers go to collect nectar from nearby blossoms.

Robert credits his fine garden pollination to the bees which are hived nearby. They help put more than honey on our table. In this day of high sugar prices, it is no surprise that many people are using more and more of nature's most perfect sweetener. It adds more than flavor and sweetness to many foods, for it helps the keeping quality, especially of baked goods. It is a great energy food. Some think it has healing qualities, and it is added to some medicines even today.

The longer Robert works with his bees the more he appreciates and understands them. It takes time and effort, but it has been an interesting hobby and helps with the food budget.

Robert now has six hives. I asked him the other day how many bees he thinks he has. With a twinkle in his eye and a big grin he answered, "The last time I counted, we had seventeen million, two-hundred thousand, and six. The six are the queens!"

We are thankful for every one.

Travel

The House Car

WHEN MY FAMILY LIVED in Madrid, Iowa, in the early 1920s, we became acquainted with a very remarkable family who lived much the same life as musicians of today who travel down the highways with their own bus. The Krantz family, father and mother and two beautiful daughters, were all talented performers. Mr. Krantz was not only an accomplished musician but an artist, designer, and woodworker as well. In the early 1920s, he had taken a Model T chassis and built upon it a "house car." Inside it had a bunk at the rear with another bunk above that divided in the middle and dropped down to form the back to make a very comfortable seating arrangement. The bunks slept the four of them nicely. A table folded against the wall during driving periods and lifted up with a supporting leg beneath it for meals. The counter arrangement was right under the windshield. A sink was sunk into this counter on the right side and a hose ran from the bottom to the outside emptied the water out of the sink into an outdoor receptacle. The steering wheel came out of the left side of the counter. In a day when trailers were unheard of and such living-on-wheels a real novelty, this house car was a masterpiece.

The Krantz family followed the concert circuit, playing a wide variety of instruments and accompanying Mr. Krantz when he illustrated the music with bright colored chalk on large sheets of poster paper. They brought a great deal of pleasure to many, many people.

When Mr. Krantz decided to build a larger "house car," one comparable in ease, beauty, and comfort to the present motor homes, my father, with the enthusiastic approval of his family, bought their little house car. Now we really had our vacation trips made. True, the vehicle could only go twenty-five miles an hour, but who was in a hurry?

When it rained, riding became a real adventure. My sister, Ruth, and I would take turns sitting on the small counter and moving the hand operated windshield wiper back and forth, back and forth. When we arrived at Lake Okoboji, or wherever our destination might be, we were then ready to pull into a camping site, don our bathing suits, and begin enjoying the place without delay. Our little house on wheels was dry, warm, everything was convenient, and we were very sure the only good way to travel was by such a "house car."

This past fall when Mother, Ruth, and I journeyed to Madrid for their church centennial, we stopped to visit at the Krantz home. Daughter Zona, who has been a special friend of Ruth's through the years and now lives and works in Ames, was home. Just as regally beautiful as ever. Mr. Kranz has his art studio in his home and still paints beautiful oils and watercolors. Mrs. Krantz, though also re-tired, retains her lively humor and keen conversational ability. As we walked from their art-filled home, we commented that the big house car should be parked outside in the drive beside the jewel of an oriental garden created by Mr. Krantz. We felt as if we could almost walk up the street to our old home and find the little original house car parked by the back porch, ready for its laughing cargo of happy people.

The Krantz family pioneered in that kind of travel years ago. I am thankful to have known them personally when they were in the most active years of their concert work.

Westward Ho

AN OLD-TIME covered wagon was never packed with more care (or more equipment) than our modern black pickup truck. Everything from the camp icebox, which our daughter Dulcie Jean insists on calling a refrigerator, to the folding cots and pup tent were tucked into the recesses of the truck box. Across the top was fastened a sturdy canvas.

Early Sunday morning, when we drove down the lane, we felt as prepared as possible to meet any situation along the western trails.

After leaving son Bob in Sidney with his grandmother Dulcy, we surveyed our maps and our crew. Dulcie Jean, almost four, and our little niece, Luanne Barnard, who will be eight years old this fall, were the junior members. Robert was unanimously elected guide and chief mule skinner, and I was drafted for the task of scribe and map reader.

Our log is full of very exciting and timely notations, such as:

10:20—Arrived in Nebraska City. Took first picture, discovering as we drove out of town that the camera lens was focused wrong. Glad it was discovered on first picture.

10:40—Dunbar, Nebraska, population thirty-six. Lovely white-framed church with many cars parked reverently in front. It inspired a long rendition of "Jesus Loves Me" by the junior members of our crew.

The countryside is beautiful and the greenest I've ever seen Nebraska in August. Still, the irrigation ditches are carrying water to see that the fine growth continues. The corn looks better than our Iowa stands. The alfalfa is deep and soft and a rich, cool green. Huge dehydrating plants are belching forth hot smoke as they turn and heat and tumble the ground alfalfa into concentrated feed.

The old sod houses are gone, but the modern, neat, red brick homes that have replaced them look substantial and prosperous. Even older houses have a wall or two cut out for a big picture window.

The countryside is dotted with television aerials, sleek cows, baled hay piled evenly into house-sized stacks, never-tiring windmills, and old, old cemeteries with dates such as 1870, 1872, 1861 imprinted on their weather-beaten tombstones.

11:15—Entered Cheney, population sixty. More grain bins than houses in evidence.

12:00—Lincoln. Finished our picnic dinner on the University of Nebraska campus. Robert went through tremendous gyrations trying to get the huge capitol building reduced into the lenses of our tiny camera. Fixed a soft pallet in back of pickup for naps. The junior members liked this arrangement so well they spent the rest of the afternoon coloring, reading, and playing with dolls in the cool interior of our covered wagon.

6:30—Found the perfect camping spot beside Lake Jackson just south of Lexington, Nebraska, for our first night out. The lake provided the girls with plenty of water for splashing and sand just right for castle building.

As the sun went down, spreading a red glow across the lake, it cast a radiance over our campers warmly snuggled into their sleeping bags and more than ready for a good night's sleep after their first day as real, rugged, outdoor girls.

Yellowstone Bears

WHEN WE DROVE INTO Yellowstone Park that year of 1951, the circulars gave us many warnings concerning the danger of molesting, teasing, or feeding the bears. We had driven two miles into the park when a line of cars parked by the side of the road proved to be congregated around two big black bears. Tourists were running in and out of their cars taking pictures, holding out food, and showing the bears to their children. They seemed completely unaware of any warning that they were near wild animals. Altogether we counted forty-one bears panhandling beside the road as we drove through the park.

Saturday evening we pulled into Mammoth Hot Springs at the northwest edge of Yellowstone. The camping area was near a big wooded stretch and not very heavily populated with tents and trailers.

Supper was underway, our sleeping bags and cots were organized for the night, and the back end of the pickup was ready for the two little girls to be snugly tucked in once supper was over. Our next-door neighbor was just coming out of the door of his trailer with a pan of food in his hand when a big black bear came loping over the hill. We hoped he was tame and liked people.

Our neighbor assured us he was a friendly bear, but said not to trust him in any way. Often bears do become fiercer if frightened or disturbed. After supper we carefully cleared away all signs of food, leaving only our heavy camp icebox under the table.

Everyone was snugly tucked in for the night. It was 11:30 when both Robert and I were awakened by a loud whomping noise. We turned on the flashlight and there in its beam, not three yards from our sleeping bags, was the huge black bear.

It was picking up our camp icebox with its strong front paws, rearing up on its hind legs, and slamming the box on the ground. That bear was determined to get the box open. We sat up in our sleeping bags, rooted to the spot. The bear gave a mighty swing, banged the box down on the ground, and the sturdy clasp flew open. We had to watch the bear eat our butter, eggs, milk, and bacon.

When he had eaten his fill, he turned his attention in our direction. Robert and I started moving, but fast. Only I became hopelessly entangled in my sleeping bag. Just as I was becoming really frantic Robert started to laugh. "You were thrashing around so wildly you frightened the bear away," he said and pointed toward the big animal lumbering up the hill.

But before he left, the bear had grabbed the two-pound lard can in his mouth. The last we saw of him he was padding off into the bushes with a bright red lard can held tightly between his teeth. As I fell back in an uneasy sleep, I knew that I preferred my bears in a zoo.

The Turtle

SINCE THE FIRST TRIP this improvised "Turtle" took to Yellowstone National Park in 1951, our family has had many travel adventures to many different places. We've camped beside roaring mountain streams, near steaming geysers, next to the blue waters of Lake Superior, and in the green woods of Iowa. Many beautiful scenes in out-of-the-way places have been available to us because of the wanderlust habits of our house in our pickup truck.

We've had lots of fun, many interesting and educational experiences, and a few wild and woolly ones! Some campsites are well equipped to make life almost as easy as at home. Since my husband is one who likes to "get away from it all" he is not interested in tile showers, adequate laundry facilities, and shelter houses with which many campgrounds are provided. He tries to locate the spots where "roughing it" is the pattern. Now that the children are a bit older, even I can view this rough and tumble life with an eye to fun and challenge.

But initially, the year we took all three of our sons high into the Rocky Mountain National Park, I wasn't at all sure this outdoor life was for me. Oh yes, we had many of the comforts of home: a garbage disposal, for instance. Every day, the garbage man would dispose of the contents of the strategically placed receptacles. Running water was to be found in abundance: cold running water from a spigot near our camp, cold running water in the wash house, and cold running water, complete with sound effects, in the rushing mountain streams.

Everyone in camp had a fireplace, that desired addition to the best establishments. It might not be as fancy as many would desire, but it did burn wood; cast heat, smoke, and ashes; and cook the food to a variety of turns. Sometimes the food would be black on one side and blond on the other. More often than not, it would be well-seasoned with pine needles. What such a fire could do to an innocent looking little egg when one's back was turned was a wonder to behold. But outdoor appetites seem to be agreeable to any type of cooking, and food disappeared with more alacrity than food gently prepared at home.

Most frequently heard words around camp: "Where is . . . ?" This applied to the salt, shortening, matches, children, a restroom, and/or a forest ranger.

Most frequent camp sound: "Klunk klunk," as each camper tackled a stubborn log. No matter how much wood was cut, it soon disappeared into the maw of the fireplace, and the camper had to go chop more. This is called "fun." It is "good exercise" and prepares one for the office, the schoolroom, the pulpit, the farm, or whatever kind of work is waiting back home.

Never will I forget the family made up of a new bride and groom and her six children by a former marriage who were headed into Canada on a combined honeymoon and camping trip. We met this unusual group in the shelter house on a rainy afternoon as they were trying to get warm and dry. The husband looked up with harried eyes and said, "I guess I should have brought along an axe."

Most common complaint at camp: "I was cold last night." This varies in intensity from the sleeping-bag-on-the-ground crowd to the snug-warm-trailer group who are loudest in talking of the cold when they rush out in the morning for a restroom stop and then rush right back in.

I try to be philosophical as I bend my knees or stoop by the fireplace to wash, rinse, or cook. Some women pay fabulous amounts for such bending exercises. Naturally, a slenderizing therapy program does not throw ashes in the face or place radiating heat at knee level, but perhaps the end results are the same.

Every year we learn more about camping. We learned, for instance, that camping with children aged eight months, two years, and six years, as we did in 1956 on our first trip to the Rocky Mountains with our three sons, is improperly called a "vacation." A vacation is supposed to be relaxing, peaceful, and calm. It is a change, however, and makes one appreciate home tremendously.

As the children grew older this kind of vacationing becomes easier. Each child has tasks to do and becomes a helper when the family is living and working together in the out-of-doors. We have learned to limit our mileage for one day. We stop often to play ball, run in a park, or enjoy the playground equipment provided in many towns. We try to stop early enough in the afternoon so that camp can get set up in a choice of places, everything can be well arranged, and supper can be eaten by about five o'clock. Nothing is more discouraging than pulling into a campground after dark and groping around to find a place to settle.

The clothing we take with us is the rough and tumble kind. I refuse to nag the children about being careful when we are living outdoors. If they get dirty, they will wash. With laundromats in so many places, the problem of getting clothes clean is diminishing rapidly.

Many of the campsites are near very fine washing and bathing facilities. Hot water, showers, and laundry rooms are increasingly being added to parks. If we go for a period of time without such a place for a good bath, we try and watch for a swimming pool. A good cake of soap, a big washcloth, and the pre-swimming shower becomes a good place for a thorough cleaning.

Dusk seems to come early across a campground. After the supper dishes are done and the children bedded down, small clusters of neighborly folks may gather around a campfire. Pots of coffee, bowls of popcorn, and cups of cocoa are shared along with friendly chatter. Away from the humdrum activities of everyday life, out in God's great out-of-doors, where nature and her creatures teach us quiet lessons of beauty, we have a chance to unwind from all our cares and worries.

We are thankful for our Turtle for getting us into such places.

Gooseberry Falls State Park

IN 1959 WE PACKED UP the Turtle, our camper on our pickup truck, and drove off to Gooseberry Falls State Park on the shore of Lake Superior north of Duluth, Minnesota. The park is a huge fifty-five thousand acres. Two campgrounds are on the lake front and two primitive camps are back in a wilderness area. A settlement called Silver City was at its entrance that contained one small general store, complete with gasoline pumps, two restaurants, a motel, and a curio shop.

The park has an abandoned copper mine, fresh springs, plunging falls, deep verdant forests, clear, cool rapids, and for the sportsman, it contains snow trails and ski runs in winter, hunting of bear, deer, and coyotes in season, and fishing for those who enjoy hiking back to the deep woods where streams flow.

All this beauty demanded exploration. The day after we settled into the campground, Robert suggested that we pack a lunch and go up one of the wilderness trails. With a lunch carefully tucked into the knapsack and carried willingly by young Bob, stick horses cut for each of the boys and walking sticks for the two older members of the party, we set out. Signs at the entrance to the hiking area told where the paths led, how far they went, and how long it would normally take to make the distance designated.

"That hike up to the falls looks about right," Robert pointed to the section of the sign which read "Falls—2 miles—1 hour hiking time one way." Merrily we started up the path which inclined sharply. The forest deepened quickly, and in a minute's time, the shore of Lake Superior was hidden from sight.

The trail was broad and firm. Hemlock, maple, birch, and pine stretched out green and brown on each side. The stillness was amazing. Not a bird call came. Not a whisper of wind blew by our ears. The scuffle of our feet was the only sound.

In the deep shade of the trees grew luxurious ferns. Moss of many varieties, from the tight-set dark green ones to the lighter colored with star-shaped tendrils, hung under fallen logs, lined the roots of trees, and edged the streams. Lichens of every imaginable color and shape clung to both the dead and living wood. The boys found one huge red fungus that looked, for all the world, like a bicycle seat. Tiny fanlike pure white mushrooms clustered in even rows on an old log. Green and brown lichens looking like delicate butterfly wings covered another.

Every few steps brought a new discovery. A green and yellow snake about one foot in length sunned himself unblinking on a log as we tiptoed past. Purple and red berries and various shades of green from the different species of trees and ferns gave the deep woods variety and beauty.

Two college boys passed us as they came back down the trail. "It's well worth the hike," they called as they hurried by. Such energy! But then, I rationalized, we pace our stride to Craig's four-year-old footsteps. Two Ohio girls came along and paused to visit and compare travel notes. We enjoyed the rest and the company. After these hikers had gone by we saw no other persons. Aside from the snake, we saw no living creature. We were deep in the wilderness surrounded by untouched virgin forest.

I thought of the tremendous courage it must have taken for the pioneers to settle in such heavily wooded territories.

We stopped to rest. The way was beginning to seem long to me. How much farther? On the map it looked like miles! I protested, but having a husband who is adamant about some things, he cajoled me into continuing to Gooseberry Falls. "You should not come this far and not go on. You wouldn't stop and play in a puddle if the ocean was just over the next hill." That moved me. On we went.

The trail grew narrow and rugged. Tree roots stood out where the water had washed down the hillside. Fewer feet had walked this way.

"I hear a waterfall," insisted first one and then another of our little group.

Around the next turn in the path we could see the water tumbling and frothing over a sharp outcropping of rock. Tamarack gave it a deep golden color. At the base of the falls and directly at our feet was a quiet brown pool. Trees rimmed the edge of the clearing where we stood.

Dropping to the ground, Robert smiled up at me. "This is it. This is the 'away-from-it-all' I've been searching for."

Then Bob gratefully dropped his pack to the ground, opened it, and brought out the sandwiches for our lunch. It became one of my most memorable meals ever.

Presque Isle, Porcupine Mountains Wilderness State Park

ONE OF MY FAVORITE camping spots is beautiful Presque Isle on the shores of Lake Superior. We had searched long to find a place which was truly quiet and remote enough to be away from traffic, crowds, and commercialism. We had camped in too many campgrounds which were bumper to bumper with people.

Since one of our reasons for camping is to get away from pressure, getting away from crowds of people is essential to our family for a true, relaxing vacation. So it was that we finally discovered Presque Isle, part of Porcupine Mountains State Park, Michigan. Here we parked our Turtle and backpacked over a mile from the end of the road to reach a swinging bridge, which took us over the Presque Isle River and onto the island itself. It was an idyllic location because the only people who made the effort to get there were those who loved the wilderness, respected it, and wanted to see it enough to walk along the trails to reach its unspoiled beauty.

It is fortunate indeed that I married a man with whom I would like to be stranded on a desert island. One thinks of such an event as far from reality in this modern day and midwestern location, but let me be the first to inform you that it can happen.

And what does one do on a deserted island? Since I now have had several days experience being the only female in such a place with four males, I can tell you that you cook, you do dishes, you put marshmallows on sticks, you plan the division of one chocolate bar to make five s'mores, you insist that you are not interested in *even one more* hike, and then, when everyone else begins to walk away and up an interesting-looking trail, you decide the heck with it. I'M not going to sit here *all alone*, and so you go along too.

You tell the smaller males that they have already set aside enough rocks to take home to pave a patio, and the Turtle can only hold so many, and then you help lug them along the trail back to the mainland. You watch indulgently as the pioneering instinct causes the boys to lash logs together and, with a crude paddle and a pole or two, you respond appropriately as they wave and set out to go to Canada to follow in the footsteps of the fur traders, or go along the coast of Lake Superior looking for a copper mine. Then you watch like a hawk to be sure they don't go beyond the safety limits. You fall into your sleeping bag at night so tired that the thought of only a thin tent wall between you and some twenty miles of wilderness doesn't matter one bit! And after you get home and look back on the experience, it seems wonderfully exciting, and you're grateful for having had it.

Undoubtedly the single most exciting incident of our stay in the wilderness camp ground at tiny Presque Isle was the night I saw the bear.

It had been a long, happy day. We had hiked far back into the forest and returned laden with fungi, pine cones, tiny green acorns, mosses, and leaf specimens. Never had supper tasted better. The large amount of fresh fried potatoes and onions was soon diminished, along with a number of salmon patties. The meal was topped off with canned peaches and cookies for dessert.

A copper-colored sun went down into the western edge of the lake as we all took one last quick dip in Lake Superior to wash off the dust of the day.

The boys were soon tucked in the tent and went quickly to sleep. Robert piled more logs on the fire. Just as the moon came up full and bright and looked as if it was standing on tiptoe on the top of a huge spruce tree, I saw a shape on the path toward the latrine. It was black and bulky and looked to be about three feet tall. As I stared at the figure, I thought I saw it move toward the underbrush.

"Robert," I nudged my husband with a sharp elbow "get the flashlight, there's a bear on the path." It seemed a long time between my urging and Robert's reaction. He finally shined the light down the path. He began to laugh. I was not amused. Having a bear near our camp was not funny.

"Oh yes it is." Robert calmed me a bit. "You are looking at a garbage can."

Can you guess what story the boys told most frequently once we arrived home? Why, the story of the night Mama saw the bear, of course.

The Black Inner Tube

THIS IS THE STORY about a big black inner tube. Now, to look at it, it doesn't appear one bit out of the ordinary. But it is different, for this inner tube belongs not inside the tire of just a car or a truck, but rather it belongs to our three sons.

On a recent August evening, the boys who belong to this inner tube were helping pack the Turtle, our pickup camper, for a summer camping trip north to Lake Superior. When it seemed that every nook and cranny was stuffed to the maximum, seven-year-old Jeff looked around to be sure no one was watching and tossed the inner tube into a corner of the Turtle and pushed sleeping bags on top of it to hide it from view.

Bouncing along in the dark and warmth of the sleeping bag-piled corner, the inner tube was carried over smooth roads and rough, over super highways and country byways.

It was not until the pickup pulled into the Porcupine Mountains State Park in Michigan that the inner tube was brought out from its hiding place. A quiet nook at the edge of Lake Superior provided enough water to float the tube. For a short time all three of our sons, plus the children from other camp families nearby, shared the excitement of sitting, floating, and paddling around in the round, floatable circle.

The inner tube was packed again, not so secretively this time, and driven along the lake to the Presque Isle State Campground. It was so primitive the road stopped about a mile from the camping area, and everything needed had to be packed in on sturdy backs. Surely this was no time to be lugging any nonessentials.

Jeff, in his own persistent way, solved the situation by announcing that he was going to the latrine. When time passed, and he had not returned, we began to wonder what had attracted his attention along the path. As we started out to look for him we met him coming into view, pulling his beloved inner tube friend behind him. He had covered the distance to the Turtle and back in record time.

Since we were the only family camping on Presque Isle, the inner tube provided excellent transportation for our three sons on the lake and in the river below the falls. Then, far more rapidly than we wished, time passed, and all too soon, it was time to lug everything back to the mainland, tuck the inner tube into the corner of the Turtle, and head for home.

We camped the following night near Hayward, Wisconsin, and the Namekagon River. It is a twisting stream, sometimes shallow, sometimes deep. After a night's rest and a good breakfast, Craig and Jeff reached inside the Turtle and brought forth their beloved friend. Playing with it like a hoop, they rolled it back and forth.

Just as Robert called, "Don't let the inner tube get away from you," the inner tube took a bounce, and moving faster and faster, rolled down a smooth steep path, past a gnarled ancient tree, over the weeds and rocks at the river's edge, and with a splash, plunked into the swift stream where it floated soundlessly, rapidly, away from us.

Three boys, weeping tears of frustration, watched their friend going farther and farther down the river. But their long-suffering father, without a word, grabbed up a big stick and rushed to the water's edge.

Telling the boys to stay on the bank, Robert ran along the path paralleling the river until he managed to get ahead of that errant tube. Stripping off his shoes and rolling up his trousers in the approved Boy Scout rescue technique, he leaped into the river at a spot where the bottom was clearly visible. He broke every speed record in grabbing the cause of all this furor!

Back on solid earth Robert handed the tube to his sons. "Take that back to the pickup, let the air out of it, and don't get it out again until we get home!" he said in a firm voice.

Yes, the inner tube and its family arrived home safely with memories of shared excitement, a flair for the spectacular, and an almost disastrous fling.

Even an inner tube can have adventures, it seems.

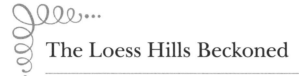

The Loess Hills Beckoned

WHEN MY HUSBAND Robert was tiny, he and his parents lived, along with sister Ruthella, on a farm tucked into a corner near the small village of Knox, Iowa.

Last Sunday afternoon Robert suggested to his sons that they go for a hike in the bluffs near Knox, just a few miles west of our home in Sidney. It did not take the younger members of the family long to indicate that this was a wonderful idea. My assignment was to stay home and prepare a big pancake supper for the hikers. With our black-and-white collie, who goes by the ridiculous name of Wheels, they piled into the pickup and drove off into one of the most beautiful fall days we've had.

The Loess Hills, which locals call the bluffs, are made up of a fine-grained, yellowish brown, extremely fertile soil that was deposited thousands of years ago by the wind. They run parallel to the Missouri river for many, many miles to form a breathtakingly beautiful part of the western Iowa landscape. They are rugged as mountains in places, though not as high. The mounds and ridges are covered, for the most part, with grass. Stretches of timber reach back in many places. Farsighted pioneers built their homes in protected areas. Enterprising people of today are erecting their homes high on the bluff tops. Rolling and swelling, dropping and rising, the view is varied and magnificent.

As the pickup crossed the few miles which separate our home from the bluffs, Robert told his sons about his own childhood in this area.

When he was one year old, his parents moved from Sidney to a small, white frame house nestled warmly under one of the protective bluffs in the community of Knox. Since the main highway from Sidney to Nebraska City went right through the town it was, indeed, a thriving center of trade. It boasted a general store that sold everything from machinery to dress goods, from groceries to kerosene lamps. A gasoline station, a blacksmith shop, a frame church (which held services once a month), and a brick schoolhouse and church (this one had a service every Sunday) were just around the curve in the road, and scattered here and there were clusters of houses which made it a bustling center of activity.

The boys were interested in every detail: the gas engine, which was very difficult to start but was essential for pumping water out of the deep, bored well, and the washing machine powered by another gasoline engine. It took their grandma all day to wash the family's weekly allotment of clothing. Farming was difficult and not very profitable for the little family. The hogs contracted cholera and died. The crops flooded out on the bottomland year after year. (Since that time, a drainage ditch has been built to prevent such constant devastation.) Many a winter the corn crop was barely sufficient to feed the horses, not a very satisfying amount, for the family needed feeding also.

Probably the most exciting experience which Robert related to his boys on the ride was the one which pertained to his running away. He was only four years old, not nearly old enough to go off by himself. His mother was busy washing when she noticed he was nowhere to be seen. She called. No answer. She called again. Still no answer! Frantic now, she rushed to the road to see if he might have wandered down the lane to the highway. No sign of him there. She had no idea which direction he might have gone.

Getting help was her only thought now. Pushing back into the timber she located her husband and father-in-law sawing wood. They joined in the search. In the meantime, Robert, oblivious to all the commotion he had caused, was wandering through his beloved woods, down into gullies, and up onto the peaks where he could look far out over the far reaches of land. Stopping to pick wildflowers and watch a brilliant butterfly, he was humming a little tune to himself when his grandfather finally, by sheer accident, saw him. Lost? Him lost? My goodness, no! He knew where he was all the time.

Never has Robert's love for the rugged bluffs or the wildlife which inhabits them diminished. Into this magic land, Bob, Jeff, and Craig were taken by their father. Knox is almost deserted now. Only a house or two remain, along with the road that still goes to Nebraska City but has long since been superseded by a highway running near Waubonsie State Park.

After spending the afternoon hiking, running, and chasing Wheels, the boys came home radiant and ready for the big supper awaiting them. Wheels arrived dragging tired with her heavy coat full of burrs and seed pods.

Robert and I sat over our cups of tea long after supper was finished and talked about the early days and how important it is to share our experiences with our children.

"They will never know exactly how it was back when we were young," Robert sighed a bit. "But we need to show them as much as we can."

Holidays

The Easter Egg Tree

EASTER, COMING AS IT DOES this year of 1956 so late in April, promises to bring a warm happy day. We are planning our Easter egg tree with the same anticipation as the last three years. So far we've blown out the eggs, tied them onto the tree branch with ribbon and with colored yarn, and taken broken eggshells and hooked them over branches and fastened them on with cellophane tape.

All of our eggs last year were prepared in the same fashion. That is, we took small sharp scissors and cut out one side of the egg carefully. (The contents of the eggs were put into a bowl and refrigerated until we could make scrambled eggs for supper.) Each shell was washed out, air dried, and then dyed. A ribbon was fastened with cellophane tape around the bottom of the shell and then brought up to make a pretty bow around the limb of the tree. The little egg baskets were filled with green artificial grass, little chickens, flowers, fuzzy bunnies, and such.

All I did with the eggs was help fasten on the ribbons. Bob's new ability to tie bows came into full use. He tied all the ribbon bows, hung the eggs on the tree branches, and helped place the tree firmly in a large green pottery flower pot. He insisted that every chicken and flower and bunny had its own special place and any suggestion from me was promptly ignored.

Bob wanted to take his tree to school, and that took a bit of doing. A big box finally solved the problem, along with Daddy's cooperation. Bob was very happy to share it with the other children in his first grade class.

One of his classmates said, "Bobby, did you help your mother make the tree?"

Bob looked disgusted. "My mother helped *me*!" he answered. And that was exactly the way it was, too.

Spring brings so much more than buds and gardens and house-cleaning! It brings the newness of life, which is Easter itself. We could well listen to the wise counsel of one of the first Native American Christians this country ever produced, who said, "Be sure not to go through life on tiptoe. Plant your foot—make a deep print!"

Craig's Halloween

SEVERAL WEEKS BEFORE Halloween, my son Craig insisted he was going to be disguised as a pumpkin head. "I'll get the biggest punkin' there is, hollow it out, and wear it on my head," he stated firmly.

When I stopped at a local grocery store to buy the pumpkins for the family jack-o'-lanterns, I told the clerk I wanted one to be a *great big one*, one large enough to fit the head of a seven-year-old.

"He'll get tired of trying to carry a pumpkin on his head," the clerk opined.

"You don't know Craig," I laughed, knowing full well if my young-est son made up his mind to move a mountain, he would get a shovel and start in, working at it tenaciously.

Just as I knew he would, he worked long and hard to scoop out the inside of that monumental pumpkin. He shaped wild eyes and a queer mouth. On the night of Halloween, he pulled an old sheet over his clothes, hefted the pumpkin to his shoulders, and then placed it over his head. He asked me, please, if I would drive him. It did seem as though his head was heavier than usual but he never complained.

Surely he had more fun than anyone. He stopped only at the homes of friends, but not one recognized him. The boy was made happy by the many who oohed and aahed and made remarks about him being a *real* pumpkin head.

With his bulldog tenacity, Craig finished the excursion with the head held high. On the way home, however, he removed it and looked up with a twinkle in his eye, "Whew! That old punkin' got heavy. Boy, I sure had fun."

Perhaps to some adults, assisting a son in his quest to be a punkin'-headed Halloween character does not sound like an exciting way of life, but I find it fascinating.

Just stick around, who knows what may happen next.

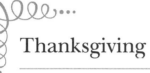

Thanksgiving

THANKSGIVING HAS A deep religious significance in our country and a long history, which makes it a truly great occasion. But, try as hard as we can, our family always gets through the reverent and serious part of the day early on, and then it ends up being a happy, festive, and sometimes uproarious event.

Thanksgiving 1951 was no exception. All of my family and my in-laws were invited up our country lane for my first effort at a family feed. We brought in the large table, which has been handed down from generation to generation. This generation uses it for eating on the porch, except for "state dinners." This venerable table has the virtue of having leaves that will extend it to enormous and sturdy length, which are two qualities a Thanksgiving table must have. After much grunting and groaning, we finally squeezed the table through the front door. We put the leaves into place and then stretched the tablecloth to its full length.

Now we were faced with a quandary. The chairs of the household would not begin to accommodate the various members of the family who would be expecting a seat at the holiday board. We finally settled by becoming good pilgrims. Robert went out to the wood piles and rustled up boxes, stumps, and planks. From these he fashioned rustic seats as basic as the ones our forefathers ever had.

Our most thankful moments of the day came when we blessed modern designers for our fine comfortable chairs. No wonder early American dinners were stern, forbidding affairs. Folks were either afraid of falling off the benches or were so uncomfortable they just wanted to eat and get out of there.

When we got the table arrangements completed, I went back to finish the preparations for dinner. Our Thanksgiving "fowls" were two huge, fat, sassy hens from the chicken yard, ones that had been unknowingly eating themselves into good, plump, seven-pound roasts. I baked them wrapped in aluminum foil, which made them all juicy and tender.

I was especially happy that I had foil under the chickens and that I had poured the drippings off early, for as the first carload of relatives drove up the lane, I dashed to the oven of the big kitchen range to give one last poke to test the meat. As I flung open the low oven door, the pan under the chickens started slipping and rather than grab it with unprotected hands, I stood looking in horror as those two large chickens slithered onto the oven door, onto the floor, and went with unerring aim across the kitchen to come to rest directly in front of the back door through which our guests would be coming at any second. Trying desperately to stay calm, I grabbed two hot pads and had everything back in place just as the first "Hello" sounded from the porch.

Regardless of such a near catastrophe, we had a fine dinner. It was an especially happy day, for it was also Robert's birthday. We had all the fun of gifts and a big cake with candles to add to our day of thankfulness.

Shopping on the Day before Christmas

HERE IT IS, one week before Christmas, and I am wondering just how everything is going at your house. Are you ready for a relaxed week ahead with all of your gifts purchased, wrapped, and under the tree or sent off with the patient mail and delivery persons?

Or do you wait until the spirit moves you? And if that spirit is a bit slow, do you still have a lot of rushing here and there to find the right gifts, need late night hours to wrap and mark, and have the biggest share of the baking still to do?

For years, husband Robert's mother did practically every bit of her preparations for the holidays on the week before Christmas. She bought and wrapped her gifts on December 24, staying up late into Christmas Eve night to finish. It became a tradition! The family insisted that it would not seem like Christmas without Grandma Dulcy's last minute rush.

It took a great deal of detective work and a huge quantity of persistence for me to ferret out the reason for this late blooming of the spirit of the holidays.

Finally, one evening, Grandma Dulcy explained that back in depression days when her three children were growing up, money was very scarce. She waited until the day before Christmas to do her shopping simply because bargains were then available. She did not plan her purchases; she bought from the stock which remained on the store shelves at that late date. Naturally, when she bought everything on the twenty-fourth, Christmas Eve was spent in wrapping her gifts.

Interestingly, my own father, Carl Corrie used to dash down to the local drug store—the only store in most small towns that carried gift items—and buy his presents at the very last minute before the great day. In contrast, my Mother Mae usually did her buying and mailing earlier but Dad's attention was involved with church programs, candlelight services, youth activities, and preparing his all important sermon for the Sunday nearest Christmas. Details like buying gifts just waited until the day before Christmas. The fact that prices were lower on that day could have influenced his timing as well.

Most years my sister Ruth, Mother, and I received a variety of kinds of stationary from Dad because the other gift items in the local drug store were sold out by the time he arrived to pursue his Santa role. His choices were usually limited to which color of stationary he should buy for which female in his household.

We all thoroughly enjoyed this yearly tradition. We vied with each other in expressing surprise and delight over the gifts. And we *were* delighted, too. We knew that Dad's love for us was the deepest, richest love a father could have for his children and his wife. His family secretly followed his joyous sprinting down to the local drug store, his fun in bringing his purchases back to the house (where he'd gather up what was left of the bright Christmas paper and ribbon), and his supposedly secret tiptoeing down to the basement with his noisy armload to wrap the gifts in the furnace room. Then he'd sneak back upstairs to tuck his gifts in the tree branches.

Do you suppose our snickers, which he never once let on he heard, gave us away?

The Sugar Cube House

WE HAVE SNOW. A lovely white, soft, filled-with-badly-needed-moisture snow fell across the heartland while we slept. The countryside is beginning to look a lot like Christmas.

Snow makes me think of Christmas, but so do sugar cubes. Every family creates holiday traditions, whether intentional or accidental, and one of ours came about in 1952 when our daughter Dulcie Jean was four years old, and son Bob was two. The December magazines were full of gingerbread houses that year (as they seem to be every year). The children brought an illustration of such a creation for me to see in the hopes that I could make one. It did not take me long to realize that if we duplicated the pictured scene, it would cost more than our entire Christmas budget. My first thought was to say no, but after a pause, I told the children it would be even better if we came up with our own design.

I'm not certain why the idea of using sugar cubes surfaced, but I did have two boxes of them in the cupboard and they looked like building blocks, so out they came, along with powdered sugar to make frosting "mortar."

First we made white powdered sugar icing and spread it over a small cookie tray to use as a base. Then we began building the walls to our house. The children had great fun slathering the frosting on the cubes (and licking off the excess). Then they placed them, one at a time, in rows to make the walls of the house. The building ended up leaning to the left, but no one cared, and the result was definitely unique.

We made the doors and windows out of stick candies and fashioned the roof out of cardboard. A cutout chimney perched on top, and with a drizzle of frosting "snow" added to our sweet creation, it looked downright festive.

The Christmas storage box provided items for the scene, and Bob and Dulcie Jean added a plastic snowman, a chubby Santa (to put inside the chimney), several artificial evergreen trees, and a little sled. They arranged these as their hearts desired, and their Christmas scene was complete.

For many years we brought out the sugar cube house for part of our holiday observance. We added to the scene. We made up stories about who lived in the house and what happened to these make-believe persons during the holidays. This tradition continued until one Christmas when we took the house down and found it worn and scraggly. We realized it had finished serving its purpose of bringing joy to our family and needed to be discarded.

The main lesson I remember about the creation of that simple decoration is that we don't have to have elaborate ornaments or fancy presents to make for a happy Christmas. Something as simple as frosting glue holding together a crooked wall of blocks of sugar, a plastic snowman, and miniature evergreen trees put together lovingly can bring great joy.

I hope you adults will have the same feeling of childlike excitement and wonder that your own children and grandchildren display, and that the feeling and love and unselfishness which you have used in preparation for the holidays will bring you the breadth of happiness which only thoughtfulness to others can provide. May you feel the glory of that first Christmas, which came through a poor family in a lowly stable during desperately fearful and troubled times.

Dulcie Jean's Four Pennies

I WANT TO SHARE two stories with you about four pennies, each involving our daughter Dulcie Jean. First a birthday story.

In 1952, when Dulcie Jean was four years old, she left home for Sunday School happily clutching four pennies in her hand. The kindergarten class she attended at the Madison Methodist Church had a plaster of Paris birthday cake with a slit in the top for putting money in and a little door in the bottom for taking it out. The birthday offerings collected were spent on special mission projects.

When Dulcie Jean arrived in the basement of the church that morning, she discovered that she only had one penny clutched in her fist.

"What did you do?" we asked her when she came up the stairs to join us for the church service and told of the loss of three pennies.

"Oh. It was O.K. I just put my penny in, took it out, and did it again 'til I put it in four times."

Her teacher agreed that Dulcie Jean had calmly solved the problem for herself. The following Sunday, she insisted on taking three more pennies to add to the amount in the bank. "They're needed," she said.

My second story happened a few months later at Christmastime. Robert, Dulcie Jean, and I left young brother Bob in Sidney with Grandma Dulcy and drove the sixty-some miles to Omaha. Our main purpose was to show our daughter the color and sights and sounds of the city at holiday time and to complete our Christmas shopping.

The thrill of choosing a gift for Bob seemed of more importance to Dulcie Jean than any of the toys she might have desired for herself. She insisted that all she wanted for Christmas was a doll and maybe a book: "If Bobby gets one too." She finally made her purchase, a bright red car which she knew her brother would enjoy. Once she paid the bill, she had four pennies left.

As we left the store, a Salvation Army helper was standing near the entrance ringing her bell and smiling at the passersby.

"What's she doing?" Dulcie Jean asked. We explained that the lady was collecting money to buy food and gifts for children who did not have much for Christmas. Immediately, Dulcie Jean smiled up at the bell ringer as she dropped her four pennies one at a time into the kettle. Robert and I added what we could and it was time to turn our attention to going home.

But the story of those four pennies did not stop there. After Dulcie Jean's death in April of 1953, we found several pennies in her little red purse.

"Do you think the bank would let us set up a Four Penny Fund in memory of Dulcie Jean?" I asked Robert.

"I doubt it. But we can add more until we have enough for their minimum requirement."

We put the pennies into a pint jar up on the cupboard shelf next to the plates and saucers and glasses that we used every day so we would see them often. Whenever we had pennies, or nickels or dimes or, once in awhile, a dollar or two to spare, we put money in the jar. When it was finally filled, we took it to the bank and told the cashier we wanted to start a Four Penny Fund. She had no idea, of course, what we were talking about, but since she was no doubt used to strange requests, she complied.

It has taken us a long time to get that fund to the place where we could do what we wanted with it. First, we added two more sons to our family, we built our house, and we got all three of our boys through college and graduate school, but we never forgot Dulcie Jean's Four Penny Fund.

What future can just four pennies have? Not much. But by adding a little at a time, those pennies grew into enough for us to provide help each year with college expenses for a deserving girl from Sidney High School.

Many decades have passed since Dulcie Jean unselfishly gave her four pennies to the church and four more pennies to the Salvation Army bell ringer, but each year at Christmastime I look for a red-garbed Salvation Army volunteer ringing a bell, and I put a check in the kettle in memory of those special moments with my sweet daughter. It is exceedingly satisfying to know that Dulcie Jean's example of love and thoughtfulness continues.

Robert's Four-Year-Old Class

WHEN ROBERT WAS teaching the four-year-old class in Sunday School the children adored him, and if he had to be away from Sidney and a substitute teacher was in charge, the youngsters were not pleased. Robert loved the children as well and taught this age group for a number of years.

One December, Robert discussed the Christmas events with the children in his class, and they created their own play in which they acted out the story. It was so pleasing that the Sunday School superintendent asked the children and their teacher if they would include the scene in the public church program being planned for Christmas Eve.

The night of the program, a tiny Mary and Joseph dressed in bathrobes and wearing towel headpieces carried a doll baby Jesus as they walked down the church aisle to the make-believe inn and knocked on the make-believe door.

"Come in," said the little boy who was acting the part of the innkeeper.

Robert was sitting on the front pew. He leaned toward the young actor and whispered, "There was no room for Mary and Joseph. When they knock again tell them to go away."

So Joseph pretended to rap on the door of the inn a second time.

"Come in," said the tiny innkeeper.

"No! No!" Robert insisted. "You don't have any room for them."

The innkeeper stamped his little foot. He put his small hands on his wee waist and threw back his narrow shoulders. "Yes I do," he answered firmly. "I made room."

Whenever I tell this story, I always end it by saying that this little boy gave us the clue to a blessed holiday. Like his version of the innkeeper, we need to make room for the Christmas child in our hearts.

The Family at Christmastime, 1969

JOYOUS CHRISTMAS GREETINGS to all of you from the family that lives up a country lane. I wish I could call it a Christmas lane, but at this writing, it has lost its snow cover and has little to make it look festive. But Christmas 1969 is overflowing inside our home. We are still busy baking cookies, writing greeting cards, and wrapping packages. We scurry around with secrets under our arms as we put them on the closet shelves and under the beds.

"Don't look in my dresser drawers," son Jeff cautions.

"Stay out of my room. I'm wrapping stuff tonight," Craig says sternly. Bob disappears mysteriously to his private corner of the basement with nothing more than a warning glance.

Our favorite recording of Christmas music, an early gift, goes on the tape player and we pile the gifts we are giving to others as a family on the dining room table. The gift wrappings and cards are passed from hand to hand as we all join in the fun. We lose the scissors and misplace the cellophane tape. Scraps of bright colored paper and the clipped ends of shiny ribbons lay scattered on the floor. Robert scoops them up and keeps the waste baskets emptied when they get full. Sometimes we forget which gift goes to which person and the tag for Aunt Ruthella's package ends up on Grandma Dulcy's. It is panic time until that problem gets sorted out.

The tree is standing majestically in the living room, filling it with Christmas. It was decorated, as has become our custom, on Craig's December 20 birthday. Bob arrived home from his sophomore year in college just in time to help with this festive beginning to our Christmas week, and to do his own preparations for the holiday.

The gifts beneath the tree are growing in number daily. It amazes me how many presents are there. Christmas in my childhood meant receiving one nice gift and perhaps an article of needed clothing. My sister's and my stockings were hung on the back of a big overstuffed chair—no fireplace in any of my childhood homes. The stockings usually held a delightful supply of hard Christmas candy, a simple toy, an orange, and some nuts. That was all. I cannot remember ever receiving gifts from aunts and uncles and cousins and very few from grandparents.

Every year I am reminded that, sadly, Christmas is not happy for everyone. Troubles and sickness and death do not take a hiatus just because it is December. Perhaps the most important gift of the season is marked for those who are in need. Christmas brings the hope of the Christ Child, faith in God's love, and His constant presence. It still brings the promise of brotherhood and peace if we will only follow the light of His star.

Someone has said that no one should be empty-hearted at the birthday of our Lord.

So we hope that wherever you are, and in whatever circumstances you find yourselves in this holy season, that your hearts will be filled with God's love, the greatest gift ever given.

New Year's, 2000

WELL, FOLKS, it is January 1 of the year 2000. We made it!

When we look at the last century, we know there are many people who cannot say that, and for those we hold near and dear to our hearts who are no longer with us, we are allowed to spend a moment or two wishing they were here to help celebrate this moment.

The closer we got to the year 2000, the more I wanted to cross over that threshold into the new millennium. Now that I have done that, I need to decide what to do with all this fresh, wonderful expanse of days stretching fresh and new ahead of me.

I've always been glad that the new year came in January when society's pressures seem to lessen, and the land itself is at rest. We have slowed down at last from the frantic haste of spring planting, summer cultivating and food processing, fall harvest, and the rush of the holidays.

And this year should be a special one. Does that mean we make more or better resolutions? For a number of years I have just gotten out the old ones, dusted them off, and then tucked them back into the drawer again to await another new year. They are still perfectly good. For example, I plan to finish sorting things in the basement and have a yard sale with the excess, I want to get my scrapbooks and photo albums up-to-date, I need to eat less sugar and fat, and I intend to plan some adventure for each month of the year. Then come the really hard ones I keep working on every year—to improve my attitude by being more patient with myself and others, to cherish my longtime friends and make new ones, and to especially treasure my younger acquaintances, for they help me have a more youthful outlook on life.

And I do, as always, resolve to do everything I can to make my little corner of the world a better place.

I have a shelf near my easy chair where I put the book I am currently reading and the ones I want to read next. As those of you who have read this column through the years know, I love poetry, so several books of verse are in that mix. It was my father who imbued in me a love of poems, for he used them frequently in his weekly sermons. I learned many as I was growing up by simply listening to him recite his favorites, which still surface in my mind at unexpected moments. The following is my favorite.

My Faith

I want the faith
That envies not the passing of the days,
That sees all time and ways
More endless than the stars;
That looks at life, not as a little day
Of heat and strife
But one eternal revel of delight.

What matters if one chapter nears the end?
What matters if the silver deck the brow?
Chanting I go
Past crimson flaming from the autumn hills
Past winter's snow
To find that glad new chapter where God's spring
Shall lift its everlasting voice to sing.
This is the faith I seek:
It shall be mine.
A faith that strides across the peaks of time.
—Ralph Cushman

So my final New Year's wish for all of you, and for myself, is a faith that truly strides across the peaks of time.

Leaning on
Everlasting Arms

Dulcie Jean's Death

OUR DAUGHTER, Dulcie Jean, was happy and a very normal child. She came home from kindergarten on April 13, 1953, complaining of not feeling well. It seemed to be only an upset stomach, no temperature, but we kept her home the next morning. At noon she suddenly went into a convulsion and lost consciousness. We rushed her to the hospital where death came quickly and quietly at 6:00 that evening. An autopsy showed only that "some kind" of virus had affected the heart muscles which accounted for the sudden attack. Added to our grief, then, was the knowledge that we would never, ever, really know what had caused her death.

We drove numbly home from the hospital through the dusk, picked up three-year-old Bob from the neighbors, and went through the motions of doing the routine chores. The long dark hours which followed were spent in communion with God and proved to be the single most strengthening factor in the days to come. God and Dulcie Jean were very close and very real that night.

Now came a day of arrangements. Grief-stricken relatives and friends had come and gone. We tucked Bob into bed and were sitting in our lonely living room. Robert finally broke the silence: "Get out the typewriter. We must write. Your column is due tomorrow."

"How can we?" I asked.

"We'll do just as you've done the many times when you could think of nothing to say—just put in a clean sheet of paper and start writing down your thoughts. Something will come."

I did not think it was possible, but together we put in the paper and began, feeling that this was one concrete way we could express our love for our daughter. The words finally did come, and together we wrote the "Up a Country Lane" column for that week.

It seems incredible but days followed days, weeks followed weeks, and soon it was years which followed years.

No one is ever really prepared for the death of a child. It was writer April Oursler Armstrong who made the statement that the greatest loneliness comes when we lose our life partner, but the keenest sorrow comes when our child dies. Her explanation, and it is a logical one, is that we never expect our children to die before we do. It is just not the proper pattern of existence! Our children should have the same opportunity to grow and develop and learn that we had. When accident or illness breaks that established routine, it is a shock beyond all comprehension.

When one has suffered such a loss, it gives him or her a feeling of oneness with everyone who suffers a similar grief. I never read of a child's death without feeling a great compassion and sympathy with the parents. Knowledge that others in similar circumstances know and care is very helpful, too. In our own experience, the notes and calls which helped the most were from people, some of whom we had never met, who had also lost children. We knew that they had a deep understanding of our feelings.

Many of these kind friends made the statement, "The pain will get better as time goes on. With God's help you will find other things to do, other people, and other children who need your help. The deep wound will heal!" I had to believe what they said; they were speaking from experience. I'm convinced now, however, that it is not just the passage of time that does the healing, for I have seen too many people grow bitter as the years go by. Rather, it is the way in which we learn to turn our loved one over to God's care and use His guidance in our own lives. It is God's love and not time which does the healing.

The friends for whom I was most grateful were those who came long after the usual period of calling had ended. The greatest need for companionship frequently comes later, after the initial shock wears off.

One friend who came to be the most help to me was a dear neighbor, Marjorie Gruber, who started coming over every Tuesday. For months following Dulcie Jean's death, she would bring her mending, her ironing, or some needlework over and spend a half-day with me. Just knowing that she would be coming each Tuesday was great therapy; she filled a painful need in my life.

How well I remember, also, feeling that I could not possibly get through one entire day. How could I get up in the morning and face a day without my beloved daughter? Then I discovered that I did not have to live the entire day all at once. All I had to do was plan and get through one minute, five minutes, one hour. Surely, with God's help, I could do that much. Jesus said it so wisely when He told us to live one day at a time and not pile on all the worries of the past and of tomorrow.

As the days passed it seemed that I managed better during the daylight hours, but the nights were still difficult. That is more simple to explain than to overcome—when one is busy and active during the day, when people are around and the radio is on, grief can be pushed more readily into the background. When the house is quiet and the body relaxed, the mind has a way of racing madly, and sorrow can become overwhelming.

One night, in the midst of a burst of grief, my husband said to me sternly (and lovingly), "You trust God all day. You are getting along fine with His help. Why don't you trust Him at night, too?" That put an entirely different perspective on my attitude.

Grief comes to each one of us in one way or another if we live very long in this old world. It can teach us compassion, love, and understanding. It can lead the way to God. The loneliness, the pain, is never completely gone—we would not want to be so callused that we could get over it or forget. But we can learn to use our sorrow, learn to share the deep grief of others, and in so doing, heal much of the hurt in our own hearts.

Dulcie Jean's Final Column

LATE ON A SUNNY AFTERNOON, September 4, 1947, Dulcie Jean Birkby opened her eyes upon the wonders and beauty of this world. She grew in wisdom—wise in the ways of caterpillars and butterflies, of baby calves and tiny lambs, of newborn kittens and romping puppies, of the creek and pasture, of the haymow and the garden. She grew wise in the ways of learning in the big brick school in Farragut, learning to read her books, to write new words, to count and color and play.

She grew in stature, tall and tomboyish with dark wind-blown hair, a pretty, sweet face, freckles on her nose, and a dimple in her chin. She ran and jumped and played with complete enjoyment. For 5½ years, she lived each moment with the same joyous enthusiasm which she transmitted so freely to others.

Her years were filled with the friendship of her neighbors, her classmates, and everyone she knew. She developed a deep understanding of the joys of sharing and helpfulness. The bus ride to school, the playtime with the children, and the talking over of her experiences with her family were special pleasures each day.

She grew in the love of her family. Her father and mother, Robert and Evelyn Birkby, her brother Bob, Grandma Corrie, Grandpa and Grandma L. V. Birkby, Great-Grandma Erie Birkby, and all the other relatives who were so much a part of her delight in life.

And, oh, how well she learned to know God. Her first trip to His house of worship was made when she was five weeks old. From then on His church became a part of her. She knew Jesus and His loving care, she knew of the plans God has for all living things, and she learned to trust and have faith in Him. Each Sunday she sang in the choir, a joyous song of praise to Him in loving confidence. And when, on April 14, 1953, her physical house was no longer fit to contain her marvelous spirit, she left its limitations behind and found in the plan of God her place in heaven, there to continue to grow in spirit, to bring peace and happiness to all who know her, and to say again, as she has said each morning as she left for school, "Be sure to meet me at the corner. I will have a kiss and a hug for you."

The Story of Two Mothers

AS I KNOCKED on the front door of a well-worn, white house, a sweet voice called out, "Come in."

I walked through the unlocked door and found myself in a small living room filled with worn furniture, knick-knacks, and memorabilia collected during years of living. Potted plants lined the window sills with one large fern that looked as if it had been in that location for decades. Handmade lace doilies covered the backs and armrests of the overstuffed chairs.

In a rocking chair beside a sunny window, with a cane leaning against her chair, sat Mrs. Knudson, whose wrinkled face, gnarled fingers, and blue-veined hands indicated that she had lived many years.

On the table beside Mrs. Knudson was a picture of a young man in an army uniform, two framed medals, and a folded American flag.

My work that year was in the Grace United Methodist church in Waterloo, Iowa. I was working primarily with the children and youth, but when my travels took me into various parts of the city, I carried with me a list of our church members who were housebound, and I enjoyed stopping in for a visit with them.

So it was on this particular day, while I was on my way to find a Sunday School teacher for a third grade class, that I knocked on Mrs. Knudson's door.

She welcomed me kindly as I told her who I was and that I had come by to get acquainted. She asked me to get a cup from the kitchen cupboard, and she filled it from her freshly brewed pot of hot tea. We sat and sipped our drinks and visited like longtime friends.

The year was 1942, and we talked about the war sweeping across Europe. She pointed to the photograph on the table beside her.

"This is my son, Jeremy," she said. "He was killed in 1917 in France. The day I got the telegram that he was dead is as sharp in my mind today as it was when it happened."

The death had occurred many years before my visit, and yet tears welled up in the old woman's eyes as she thought of her lost son. She was a mother crying for her child with a memory as painful as when his death had taken place.

I have never forgotten that moment, for I shed sympathetic tears for a young man I never knew, with a mother I had just met. I realized for the first time the pain of losing a child continues for a lifetime.

Fast forward to April 14, 1953, in a simple country home many miles from Mrs. Knudson. It was at Cottonwood Farm, located south of Farragut, Iowa, where on a bright April day my husband Robert and I sat mourning the unexpected death of our five-year-old daughter, Dulcie Jean. As I sat thinking of our loss, my mind went back to the day in Waterloo when I first came face to face with the deepest grief I had ever seen. Now I was experiencing the same kind of sorrow myself.

Now, over fifty-eight years since our daughter's death, I am the mother sitting in a rocking chair with a handmade doily across the back. I am the one with wrinkles on my face, gnarled joints in my fingers, and blue veins across the back of my hands. Thankfully, I do not need to use a cane. I can move easily enough to make myself a cup of tea. But just like Mrs. Knudson, I look at nearby photographs of my daughter and realize that grief is always close. The memory of my child's death, like hers, is sharp and painful and tears fall.

The day I shared my new friend's sorrow, she became an important person in my life. Without realizing what she was doing, Mrs. Knudson offered me a rich learning experience that has helped me, years later, through my own deep, shadowy valley of despair.

The Return to Farragut of One of Its Boys

A SMALL, LITTLE-NOTICED ITEM was in the newspaper last week telling of the return to Farragut of one of its boys. It is the kind of an item that could bear much reading between the lines. The story would be far more worthwhile than many of the accounts of juvenile delinquency or youthful indiscretions that frequent our newspapers.

This story might start like this: Once upon a time a baby boy was born in a big rambling white farmhouse set on top of a high hill north of Farragut, Iowa. The house looked down into the valley that holds the East Nishnabotna River and the small rural town of Farragut, then peered across to the distant hills to the south and west. It is one of the loveliest views in southwest Iowa. Here, the growing boy roamed the hills, learned about the trees, grasses, and insects in the timbers, collected quantities of treasures which are of utmost value to small boys, and happily flew kites in the green meadow.

When school started, he would run laughing and skipping out of the big white house, chasing his sisters and running a race with his brothers to see who could reach the school bus first. Then came the ride into town with the other boys and girls who found him a happy, fun-loving companion. Oh, he was full of mischief. Who would want a boy who didn't tease and play pranks once in a while? But with all his fun, his enjoyment of sports, and the outside activities of the school, he worked hard, studied, and learned the ways that help him to do well any project he attempted.

As with most farm boys, he helped with the chores, first just tagging along with his father and older brother. Then came the time when he could carry the empty buckets, and finally, he was old enough to be trusted with the baskets full of precious feed for the waiting animals. Gathering eggs may not have been a very exciting job after the first week, but it helped teach him a sense of responsibility and helped him develop the ability to carry through and finish necessary tasks.

The church figured prominently in his life. On Sunday and during the summer when Vacation Bible Schools were being held, he always attended. He learned the place of God in this great universe and made Him a part of his life. He stood with the white-robed Junior Choir and sang joyously at Christmas programs, the Easter services, the day the entire group practically became members of the church, and even the sad day when they sang at the funeral of their dear friend and minister, the Reverend Carl Corrie, who had taught them the ways of religious living and brought them into the fellowship of the church.

There is much more to the story. His high school days, the girls he dated, the lasting friendships made, the months of working in nearby Shenandoah, and finally his enlistment in the army in 1950.

When he came home in February of 1953 the other day, he brought with him the war in Korea. No longer was it a fight in a faraway land. It became a battle close to Farragut. Heartbreak Ridge was not just a name used in a radio commentary or on a map. It became a place full of service, sacrifice, pain, and suffering.

The newspaper item was brief. It said that "The body of Dwight D. McMahon, 21, son of Mr. and Mrs. Hal McMahon, who was killed in fighting on Heartbreak Ridge October 26, was returned to Farragut last week. A short memorial service was held Sunday at the Methodist church."

That was all. But those of us who could see behind the words knew that Dwight was home at last.

Grandma Mae Corrie

(My mother, Mae Corrie, died at the age of ninety on March 24, 1972. Her grandson, Bob Birkby, wrote this accolade to his grandmother and I used it in my "Up a Country Lane" column the following week.)

I BELIEVE IT HAPPENED on the seventh day while God was resting. He had just spent the week making all of creation, and it was really mankind's first birthday. Now as God was taking his morning shower, he suddenly realized that he had forgotten to give man a birthday present, so he put on his slippers and robe, sat down at his huge desk, and pondered a great heavenly ponder. Suddenly his face brightened. He threw back his head and laughed a deep friendly laugh and sat smiling at his own wisdom, for he had devised the most pleasing, satisfying gift men could receive. He would give them grandmothers.

Everyone should have a grandmother or two. They were created to fill a very important role for children. They know more about little folks than mothers ever do, understand the trials and tribulations of tiny tots long before fathers can, and they make the best oatmeal cookies and cinnamon rolls in the world. Young salesmen can depend on their grandmothers to support blossoming sales careers by buying Christmas cards, raffle tickets, Girl Scout cookies, and magazine subscriptions, even though they don't need them. They can be trusted for the security of a birthday dollar, and no one weathers childhood without at least one of grandma's embroidered pillowcases and a dozen hand-stitched handkerchiefs. A shirt isn't really a shirt until grandma has sewn the buttons back onto it.

A grandmother lives in a magic house, though only her grandchildren can sense and appreciate its mystic qualities. Her home smells different, warm, and safe like baking, with worn furniture and fading pictures stirred together. The floors always creak, the candy dish is never empty, and there are a thousand secret hiding places not even grandma has discovered. The rooms are small, just right for a little guy and his grandmother, and within these rooms and between these special relatives, every secret is safe, every story is heard to the end, every ambition is encouraged, and dreams become realities. Time stands suspended between the divided generations.

While searching through stories and pictures, the grandchild is filled with hopes and wants, churning with a desire to know the past and transform his legacy into the future. She has lived long enough to know nothing is impossible, that the obstacles of most dreams are surmountable. She watches knowingly as her grandchildren struggle with life, for she has a special trust that they will succeed.

As with all gifts, grandmothers eventually wear out and are put aside in a special corridor of the mind. Even after the last cookies have been eaten and the final pillowcases have become faded and worn, the simple encouraging faith of a grandmother remains. Whether she is near or not, if a grandchild has just once felt the security of her unquestioning love, he can face his world a little more bravely.

Thanks once again, God. You did a nice job. We all need to feel wanted and needed, and no one can do that quite like a grandmother.

—By Bob Birkby

Grandpa "Shorty" Birkby

THE SUMMER MY HUSBAND Robert added a garage and a porch to our house, we discovered Grandpa "Shorty" (Lawrence Virginius Birkby) was our major observer and critic. Not a crooked nail or a sawed board escaped his eagle eye. Each evening he and Grandma Lucretia would drive the few blocks which separated our homes to check the progress.

When the combination screen and storm windows were finally in place, Shorty was delighted. He sat for long hours on the porch and visited with whoever was at hand. It was "his" porch. Craig came home from college and spent much time with Grandpa telling him about his upcoming medical training. Jeff came home and brought boxes of slides taken during the family's July canoe trip. On Labor Day weekend, Jeff planned a showing of his spectacular pictures. Naturally, the event had to be held on the new porch.

Shorty's sister, Mildred Reade, and her husband, Jimmy, came to see the slide show. Shorty and Lucretia's daughter, Ruthella, with her daughter, Luanne Mannon, with her three daughters, Kelley, Mollie, and Emily, and all the rest of us who live in the area came. The porch bulged.

As Shorty beamed to have all the people he loved so much around him, Jeff projected his views of Montana, the Missouri River, and our family vacation. Luanne brought out her slides of a just completed family trip to Disneyland. It was a wonderful evening.

The following Monday was a fine, sunny day. Grandpa worked in his yard in the morning and visited with members of his family who dropped by. In the afternoon, while sitting in his comfortable overstuffed chair in his living room, talking with wife Lucretia and daughter Ruthella, Shorty suddenly gasped, laid his head back on his easy chair, and closed his eyes.

His son Robert was working right across the street and came immediately when his mother and sister telephoned. The efficient Sidney rescue unit arrived soon after. Orderly, as he had lived, Grandpa Shorty died.

The patriarch of the family is gone. He will be greatly missed.

Grandma Lucretia "Dulcy" Birkby

(My son Bob was asked to say a few words on behalf of the family of his grandmother, Lucretia Isabella Carter Birkby, nicknamed Dulcy by her children, for her funeral in the Methodist Church in Sidney, Iowa, November 21, 1998. His talk translated into the following column.)

LUCRETIA'S WAS A remarkable life in many ways—remarkable for its richness, for its simplicity, for all that she accomplished among us. Remarkable that she did all of that in a full century of living—within a half mile radius of this very spot in Sidney, Iowa.

She was born in 1898 in the house just across the street from this church. In fact, when she was born, this church had not yet been built. When she was five years old she could have looked out the window of her house and watched the construction.

The streets of Sidney were still dirt roads, crowded with buggies, wagons, and mules. No automobile had ever driven around the courthouse, no airplane had flown overhead, and no one in Sidney had ever made a phone call.

She graduated from high school a couple of years before Sidney's new high school building opened. She married, and two years after that, in 1918 a terrible flu epidemic swept across America, killing thousands. Lucretia was nine months pregnant when she became gravely ill. A physician said that she would not survive her baby's birth, but she lived anyway and gave birth to son Robert, the first of three children. Then, as if to prove how wrong the doctor had been, she lived with such robust health that she didn't stay overnight in a hospital until she was well into her nineties.

Ours is a family of tremendous humor and many practical jokes. While I don't recall Lucretia every playing pranks on others, she was often the target. While many members of Lucretia's family achieved significant height, she herself was not what one would call the tallest vine on the trellis. After church, a favorite trick of family members taller than Lucretia, which was almost all of us, was to gradually gather around her until we were standing shoulder to shoulder and boxed her in. Then we would ignore her and talk among ourselves over her head. She was pretty wily, though, and usually saw that one coming a mile away.

Sometimes when we were being more serious, we would ask her to tell us about things that had happened to her earlier in her life. Almost always she would say, "Oh, I don't know why you want to hear about that old stuff."

But there were times when she did allow her history to come pouring out, mostly on summer evenings when we would all be sitting on the porch snapping beans or shelling peas—getting work done, you understand, so it was okay to visit—all sorts of Birkbys and Barnards and Carters and whatever shirttail relatives were around. For hours, against the drone of June bugs and the flash of fireflies, the stories would unfold, and Lucretia would be in the middle of the telling —who had lived where, what Sidney buildings were now gone, dates of events, details of marriages, births, deaths, eyewitness descriptions of blizzards, floods, fires, the whole give and take of human affairs in Sidney, Iowa, for as long as anyone could remember, which in Lucretia's case was a very long time indeed.

On winter evenings after family dinners at her house, she would sometimes get out The Box, a cardboard box filled with old photographs and letters and documents. We would pass them around the table one by one, and each would set off a string of stories—stories that made us aware of how Lucretia and our family and the other people of Sidney and Fremont County had become so tightly woven together over the course of all these years.

Among my favorite photographs in the box were black-and-white images of Lucretia as a child—the one where she's wearing a huge bow on top of her head, the one of her sitting on a sled in the snow with her sisters and brothers, the formal family portrait with the stern-faced adults holding still for the photographer while Lucretia, no doubt acting up again, is a bit blurry in the front row. In every one of those pictures, she is full of energy and life. And in every photo she has a very mischievous grin. If you ask me, she looked like trouble.

I think she would be charmed to find us all here today and embarrassed by all the attention. Well, Lucretia, what we are doing here is acknowledging our sadness that you are no longer with us. We are mourning the loss of so beloved a relative, neighbor, and friend. We are here to celebrate a life well-lived, and to reconfirm that what you gave to so many of us continues to warm our hearts and give us hope for the future. Even in your last years as your health failed, you often brought a joy and a lightness of being to each day.

Last April first we gathered to celebrate Lucretia's hundredth birthday. Many of you were there that day, and it was a very sweet occasion even though we nearly burned down the health center when we lit the hundred candles on the cake. Lucretia was delighted to spend time with so many people who had been part of her life. As we were leaving, she waved from her window and gave us a little smile.

And I think if she could, that is what she would leave with us today—a smile, a little wave—and then she would be on her way at the completion of this most unassuming and worthwhile life.

Not that she wouldn't have also been a little mischievous right at the end. And maybe she was. On the night that she died, there was a meteor shower, one of the largest in this area's living memory. It would be just like Lucretia to tell us not to make a fuss about her dying, and then to go off in a shower of stars.

—By Bob Birkby

My Sister Ruth

THE LAST CHAPTER of my sister Ruth Corrie Bricker-Gerhardt's life was played out last Saturday, July 24, 2010, in the Farragut, Iowa, cemetery.

Ruth died on July 4, and in the modern tradition of choosing cremation, which Ruth did, it meant that her son Larry could take time to plan her memorial and arrange it so his son Corrie and his family could attend the Iowa services.

Ruth had lived the first years of her married life to Oliver Bricker in the Farragut area, so it was appropriate that part of her ashes be brought back here to place beside Oliver.

Jeff was the first relative to arrive, coming from Missoula, Montana. Then Larry, Ruth's son, got to Sidney from his Mesa, Arizona, home on Friday just in time for the sweet corn feed at the Fremont County Fair. It was a nice reintroduction to Iowa and its pattern of celebrating the growing season of one of our most famous food crops.

Corrie, Larry's son, and his wife Krista and children, Araelyn and Aiden, took a red eye flight out of Phoenix so as to arrive on Saturday morning, the day of the service. They settled into the new downtown hotel in Shenandoah for a morning nap before it was time to gather in the afternoon with friends and family at the Farragut United Methodist Church for a traditional midwestern memorial service.

I was reminded anew as I walked into the familiar Farragut sanctuary, how comforting flowers can be and why they are part of memorial services. The baskets and vases of blossoms at the front of the church were beautiful. Our area florists are true artists in the way they put together colors and shapes and sizes of various blooms.

I don't have a clue what other people think of as they wait for a funeral to start. I usually think of those of my family and friends who have gone before. That day I remembered other memorials I had attended in this same church—many shared with my sister in presenting the music for the event. Our father's funeral was held here. He had been the pastor of this church for four years before his death and often said they were the happiest years of his ministry.

The light streamed in through the stained glass windows as pianist Terry Stafford added his remarkable musical talent to Ruth's service. He played a number of selections that were her favorites. I kept my emotions under control until he began the melodies for some of the numbers Ruth played on her violin and all the memories of time together came flooding back into my mind. "They are precious memories," I told myself as the Reverend Jaye Johnson began his excellent sermon that emphasized the many good works that were part of Ruth's life during her active years.

As Ruth had requested, Terry played "When the Saints Go Marching In" to conclude the service. How appropriate.

As we left the church to go to the cemetery for the committal service, we heard a bit of thunder and saw clouds overhead. But our umbrellas weren't needed; the sky cleared, the clouds disappeared, and the sun began to shine over the quiet rows of stones marking the graves of many of the people Ruth knew well when she lived nearby. Neatly mowed grass surrounded the wreaths and flowers on some of the graves, showing that there are people who care.

We added the wreath that my family had the florist prepare for this purpose to Ruth's grave. It held lovely white flowers interspersed with orange blossoms, for Ruth loved orange. Then those who loved her best gathered to send her homeward. Reverend Johnson read a scripture and then gave a closing thankful-for-her-life prayer, and all of us who loved her and were gathered there said, "Amen."

As is the tradition in midwestern communities, Ruth's friends and family returned to the church for coffee and cookies and a time to visit. Larry had put together an amazing DVD with a series of photographs of Ruth at various ages plus a background of her favorite music. He had added a series of photographs to the bulletin board at one side of the room to highlight her experiences.

As we bid goodbye to our friends, we felt a strong sense of love surrounding us. Close church and community ties are a great comfort at times like this.

A Country Church in Winter

IF YOU TAKE THE gravel road that goes south past our Cottonwood Farm, drive two miles over rolling hills, past clean, well-kept farmhouses, near fields spotted with snow and pastures cold and brown, you will come to the small white frame Madison Methodist Church. Just east of the church are picnic tables that in summer are often laden with rich well-prepared country food and surrounded by happy, laughing, sun-tanned faces. Now the tables are cold and uninviting, lonesomely waiting for the time when the church pot lucks and ice cream socials can again be held under the big elm trees. It is a country church just like so many that dot the rolling hills from east to west in our nation.

This very church was the place of one of the most valuable lessons I ever learned. In 1940 my father was minister on a two-point circuit, which included this Madison Church (the other church was in Farragut). He loved the church with its high-held bell and found its strong sturdy hard-working folk a constant challenge and inspiration. One cold icy late December Sunday morning at the close of the service in town, Dad asked me if I would like to drive out to the Madison church with him for their eleven o'clock service. I was appalled to think he would try to navigate the ten miles on the ice- and snow-packed narrow-graveled road. He just gave me a look, made no reply, and started for the car. Not to be outdone, I climbed in beside him.

We slid and slithered carefully but safely down to the little white church. When we walked in the door we were greeted by four people. I turned to Dad in amazement, "We might as well go home. Five people don't make a congregation."

"Each person here made a sacrifice to come. They came because they had a need. Who am I to be too proud to preach to them because their number is few? Some of Jesus' greatest sermons were to only two or three people." With that, Dad walked up to the pulpit.

I shook my cold fingers to regain some feeling and played the piano for the hymns. Then the five of us sat on the front row next to the register and listened to the greatest sermon I ever heard my father preach.

The wind was blowing icily as we walked out the wide door of the church. It was good to get into the car where the cold was not as cutting. We drove some distance in silence, and then Dad spoke. "Remember, Evelyn, it is never the number of people with whom you work, but what you give the ones who come that really makes what you do a success or failure."

Little did I know that day that I had heard my father preach for the last time. The next day, I left Farragut to return to my teaching duties in northeast Iowa. Just four weeks later, on February 1, Dad suffered a severe infection and left for a richer pastorate, but the lesson he taught me on the icy trip we made out to his country church is as true today as it was then. It is what you give to others that makes life a success or a failure, not the size of the gift you give or the number of those who receive.

In Sickness and
in Health

OVERLEAF
Our wedding, Sidney Methodist Church, November 3, 1946.

The Wedding of Robert and Evelyn

"IT'S ABOUT TIME," said Robert's mother Lucretia, "I began to think Robert would never get married."

"I've got to go to work." Robert's father, Shorty Birkby, waved as he went out the door. "Anything you plan is all right with me."

"Thank goodness!" my mother Mae Corrie stated. "I'll help make the wedding gown."

"No matter what you do, you'll never catch up with me on wedding anniversaries," chuckled Robert's brother Jack.

"Sure, I'll be your bridesmaid and help with my son Larry's responsibility as ring bearer and daughter Luanne's as flower girl," Robert's sister Ruthella nodded.

"I'll be glad to be your matron of honor. After all, you did the honors at my wedding," smiled my sister Ruth. "How about me having one of the dinners at my house?"

"I'd like to perform the ceremony," volunteered the Reverend Alvin Maberry, Shenandoah's Methodist minister.

"It would be nice if I could play the organ," suggested Marie McMichael of the Shenandoah Church. "After all, you'll be living here in Shenandoah."

"I'll bake the cake and head up the reception," offered Estelle Hopkins, president of the local WSCS. "The Women's Society of Christian Services of the Sidney church always thought a lot of your family."

"Yes, you can pick gold mums out of the trial gardens for your decorations," the May Seed and Nursery Center manager kindly consented. "They will soon be frosted and gone anyway."

"You need greens for the background," a farmer friend south of

Farragut suggested. "We have long-needled pines which would be perfect. Come get all the branches you want."

Robert's landlady Hazel Martin laughed happily, "Glad I could help serve as cupid. Robert is our favorite roomer."

Dr. Goff was the minister for whom I was working in Chicago when I made the decision to come back to Iowa to marry Robert. He was not happy that I was leaving my position as Director of Youth Activities at the First Methodist Church.

"Evelyn, you can't leave your work here at the Temple. You don't know what you are doing. This marriage will never last."

Fanny Jay, whose hometown was Shenandoah, had been a professional worker in the Methodist church for years before her retirement. She, too, felt I was wasting my life by leaving church work for marriage.

Despite all the confusion, on November 3, 1946, Robert and I stood in front of the altar of the Sidney Methodist Church and recited our vows. Al Maberry guided the ceremony, organist Marie McMichael played Liszt's "Liebestraum," and Estelle Hopkins provided the cake. Five-year-old Larry and three-year-old Luanne performed nobly in their appointed roles.

The only sad part of the moment was the fact that my own minister father, Carl Corrie, who died in 1942, was not present to give me away and perform the ceremony. Since I was perfectly capable of giving myself away, I decided to walk down the aisle alone.

No, the minister did not ask, "Who giveth this woman to be married to this man?" Mother agreed that I was in complete charge of this project and was not being "given away."

The wedding reception turned into a gala party. Leeman Jackson, Robert's lifelong friend and classmate, brought a live duck in an appropriately wrapped package marked "a box of quackers." This was in the days of simple weddings, and our guest list of about a hundred meant that the gifts could be placed at one side of the church dining room where we opened them at the reception. The guests were delighted with the arrangement, especially when one furious quacking duck emerged from its prison.

Reverend Maberry sang some happy romantic songs, and as Robert remembers, punch cups clinked, people ate cake, visited, laughed a lot, and it was all great fun.

The day had been gloomy and overcast when we went into the church, but just as we emerged, the sun came out to create a magnificent red and gold sunset. It was a good omen; I felt God's blessing on our marriage.

And both Dr. Goff and Fanny Jay were proven wrong.

During the years that have passed since these two made their predictions, I have looked at Robert and our children and smiled. A waste? Oh, I think not. It was an advantage for me personally in so many ways and, I trust, for the corners of the world in which our offspring reside. It is true that love and loyalty alone can make for a lasting and event-filled marriage.

The Night the Bed Fell on Our Honeymoon

HAVE YOU EVER READ James Thurber's story "The Night the Bed Fell"? It is well worth finding in the famous humorist's books, or you can discover this particular story on the internet. It is a hilarious tale of the time the bed fell on his father.

Now, in the big scheme of things, with the current stability of most beds in current use, beds falling down may well be a lost art. I have, however, a story about such an experience which I have never told to anyone. Not ever. Not until today.

It happened on our honeymoon in the Basin Park Hotel in Eureka Springs, Arkansas. We had spent our wedding night in St. Joseph, Missouri, and then had driven down to Eureka Springs the following day. It was late when we arrived and raining, so we were pleased to find the Basin Park Hotel open for business. Since it was the first week in November, very few people were enjoying the atmosphere and attractions of this fine, unusual historic town.

The hotel was built in 1905 near the bottom of the hill upon which the city is built. It advertises the fact that each of its nine stories is on ground level, for it is built into the side of a mountain and has an exit onto the rock face that stands behind it. Built of local limestone, it is a unique addition to the Basin Park where the original mineral spring still bubbles. Native Americans used that spring first, along with other springs in the area, and now the park is a sweet, gentle place surrounded by more rocky outcroppings, and bordered by the elegant hotel.

No one else, it seemed, was staying in the hotel that night of our arrival. Robert and I were ushered up the creaking elevator to find our room a large one at the front of the hotel. It held three double beds. As we beheld the spaciousness and the fact that the place could sleep our entire extended family, we asked one another if we should stay three nights so as to try out all three beds, sort of like Goldilocks and the three bears.

"You choose," I said to Robert, showing a kind cooperative attitude to my new husband. "Let's take that one," he pointed to the middle bed.

Now you need to realize that many beds in those days had slats. These were boards that were laid from one side of the bed frame to the other. The springs and mattresses were then placed on top of the boards.

Sometimes the slats were just a tad short. If this happened, the springs and mattresses were not in the sturdiest of positions. But we didn't know that. The following morning dawned bright and cheerful, and I awakened first. I went over to the window to look out on the stone buildings across the winding street and reveled in the sense of joy in this interesting place at this moment in my life.

I looked over at my sleeping husband. Without giving it a second thought in what I was doing, I ran over and jumped on the bed beside him. The slats slipped. The boards went down. The mattress and springs followed as the entire bed came crashing down to the floor. We found ourselves in a confusing muddle of legs and arms and blankets.

I looked apprehensively over at Robert. Would he be angry with me? Would I get the first scolding of our married life? But he was smiling. Soon he laughed out loud. Oh joy! What a wonderful man I had married!

And that, good friends, is my story of the time the bed fell on our honeymoon.

Years later Robert, son Jeff, and I returned to Eureka Springs to find the Basin Park Hotel still standing. It has gone through a number of metamorphoses since that night so long ago when we spent the second night of our honeymoon in that spacious room.

Jeff had made reservations for us and we found ourselves ushered up the same creaky elevator into a lovely room with Arts and Crafts patterned wallpaper and fabric and Frank Lloyd Wright style lamps. Robert looked it over carefully and then pulled up the bedspread so he could examine the frame carefully.

"This is one sturdy bed," he stated. "An entire box is built under the springs and mattress. I'll guarantee it will stand firm and sturdy."

And it did. But I was a little sad. While we reprised our 1946 visit to Eureka Springs, the funny experience of being in a bed that collapsed will probably never happen again.

Marriage: The First Ten Years

(On November 3, 1956, Robert and I celebrated our tenth wedding anniversary. In honor of this occasion, I wrote the following column.)

THE TALL WALNUT TREE stood as a sentinel above the grassy green glade. Surrounded by other trees, on a high rise of land and separated from all vestiges of civilization, it was a perfect place for a romantic picnic. That evening in July of 1946 was beautiful. As dusk fell, the moon rose full and white. The campfire glowed. The words of the poem were perfect with such an accompaniment of soft moonlight, flickering firelight, and quiet woodland noises. "A trail's end, a cabin, a bit of blue sea! These are the things which mean heaven to me!"

A romantic setting? Indeed it was! Whether it was the fine lacing of the leaves of the walnut tree, the moon, the tasty chicken dinner, or the poem, the combination proved most effective and Robert proposed marriage. No longer could we two who shared that scene say we were searching for the trail's end. We had found it.

But it wasn't really a trail's end at all. It was really just the beginning. The second scene of this scenario took place four months later in November of 1946. The Methodist church in Sidney had never looked more lovely, and the candles had never shown as bright. Although more beautiful brides and more handsome grooms probably walked those aisles, no one could convince Robert and me that that might be the case. With all the hopes and dreams which a wedding day carries with it, with the glow of youth, with the promises of a wonderful life ahead, we heard the preacher speak the final words, "I now pronounce you husband and wife. Whom God hath joined together, let no man put asunder."

How could the years have passed so rapidly? Now we are celebrating ten years together. How could they contain so much? How much wiser I am now than I was then. Living in close proximity with someone else makes self-examination strangely necessary and often painful. Glimpses of insight come quickly when viewed through another person's eyes and another's background.

Much is said about "adjustment" in marriage, and what a multitude of experiences that one word covers. "Adjusting" means learning the way each person likes breakfast prepared, the kind of toothpaste, the hour of rising, the number of blankets on a cold night, window up, or window down!

Evidences of true adjustment are easy to spot. When an evening is long and compatible, although not one word is spoken over newspaper and book, when one can walk into the room and sense immediately if something is wrong, or something is good, you are adjusting. Adjustment comes when the romantic dreams of youth turn into a deepening, enriching love, which is not a possession of the very young.

Ten years of marriage hold many things. Broken plumbing, scooping snow, myriads of dishes to fill, scrape, and wash, clothes to wash and dry and iron, floors to scrub and wax and dust, hot stifling nights, and cold chilling days. Ours included putting up hay, milking cows, wading in mud, plowing and planting, gardening, and canning.

Our ten years have held four dashes to the hospital for a baby's birth. We've had the fun of watching baby smiles, wobbling footsteps, a little girl rocking her dolly, little boys pushing their tractors, and hearing words as tiny minds developed. We have found that we have gained the most as we shared home and love with each new member. Of course they've brought demands on mother and father, splinters and bumblebee stings, flu and measles, and nights spent worrying over feverish little ones. (The marriage ceremony does not mention these things!)

It has been an accumulation of memories. Ten years of Christmases, ten years of Thanksgivings, ten years of birthdays, along with programs and school buses, singing songs and drawing pictures, laughter and humor, and fun in great quantity. Ten years of sharing religion: kneeling by tiny beds, teaching and singing, working together and worshiping in the church together, sharing the stories of the Bible, discussing our own thoughts about God, trying to live in the path Jesus set for those who love him, dedicating our little ones to God before they were ever born, and giving one of them, with confidence, back to the creator who sent her. Yes, ten years of reminders that nothing can separate us from the love of God.

How grateful we are for these years of learning to know how wonderful a marriage can be. And the poem I recited that beautiful July evening ten years ago when Robert proposed to me still holds true:

Trail End

A trail's end, a cabin, a bit of blue sea!
These are the things that mean heaven to me!
And what does it matter, how humble, how far,
Just so I may find them, wherever they are . . .
What more can I ask, save an old song or two,
And a trail end that leads in the gloaming to you.
—Cristel Hastings

Thirty

Thirty-Five Years Remembered

AFTER ROBERT AND I had been married for ten years, our contemporaries went to Las Vegas for a week of fun. I wrote a column about all the valuable lessons marriage had taught us along the way, washed up the diapers, tucked our sons into Grandma Dulcy's house, and Robert and I drove down to St. Joseph, Missouri, to relive a few of the romantic moments of our honeymoon. Sadly, the hotel where we spent our wedding night had been torn down, and the supper club where we ate our first meal together as husband and wife had turned into a bar and grill. So much for returning to the romantic scenes of ten years before.

When we had been married for twenty-five-years, our contemporaries were going to Hawaii. We looked in the mirror in amazement at the changes the years had wrought, dolled up in new square dance clothes, welcomed oldest son, Bob, home from college (he rode his bicycle all the way from Sioux City to Sidney for the event) and, along with younger sons Jeff and Craig and other assorted relatives and friends, had a square dance anniversary party.

Now we have reached the thirty-five-year milestone in our lives together. Our contemporaries are going on Caribbean cruises, tours of England, Scotland, and Wales, and journeys to Switzerland. We find ourselves at this moment far too busy to write a column about any valuable lessons learned, have a party, or even to look in the mirror. Craig is still in college in Iowa City, Jeff is living in Helena, Montana, and Bob is writing in Seattle, Washington—no chance for a bicycle ride home this time. Robert and I plan to celebrate by putting on our oldest clothes this November 3, to try something entirely new.

After all these years, we told each other we should be old enough and daring enough to take on a brand new challenge. So we decided to install wallpaper on one of the rooms in our house. One of the local merchants helped give us directions and assured us we should have no problems. Friends informed us that they had had such experiences for years, and two sisters from Randolph earn their living by putting on wallpaper.

And so we bought wallpaper, paste, and cutting utensils, set a time to rent a steamer, and began to have doubts.

The first concern surfaced when my good friend, Virginia Miller, told me that she and her husband Warren almost parted the day they tried to wallpaper together. The paper went on crooked, and it seems Virginia insisted that if Warren had done the measuring more carefully, it would have been straight, and they would not have needed to do it over.

And so we stripped off the paper which had been firmly adhered to the wall for eighteen years. I kept out of Robert's way until he was almost covered with damp, sticky paper. Then I scooped up the stuff, swept, and wiped until all the wallpaper he had removed was in the trash. Then we repeated the process as we moved around the room.

All went well until Robert hit a stretch that I had repaired several years ago. Now he was faced with two layers of paper and a white glue-like substance which defied all efforts to remove. It took two and one-half hours of steaming to do a four-foot square of wall. If the library had not by then been closed, I would have gone over immediately and tried to find a book on "How to Wallpaper for Beginners."

The work progressed despite our amateur efforts. The wall is clean, coated with what I think is really an undercoat but is called "sizing," and it is waiting. We have chosen November 3, our thirty-fifth wedding anniversary date, to finish the installation. But just in case our happy marriage totters on the brink as the papering progresses, I have two nice steaks, a loaf of homemade bread, and a make-ahead salad all ready to bring out at the peak psychological moment when the last piece of wallpaper is in place. One thing I've learned in these thirty-five years: man does not live by bread alone, but a good meal can soothe many a frazzled nerve.

Sixty-Four Years and Counting

"YIKES!" I said when I got up this morning.

"Yikes!" Robert said when he looked at the thermometer and saw that it recorded zero degrees at 7:00 A.M.

"Yikes!" we both said when we looked at each other across the breakfast table. "Can it be?"

And it was. November 3, 1946, the momentous day in our lives when Robert and I were married sixty-four years ago. Sixty-four years had passed since that day. Now it was November 3rd, 2010. No wonder we said "Yikes!"

"What anniversary days do you remember?" I asked my patient husband.

"Let's see. Last year we—" And neither one of us could remember anything special we did for our sixty-third year together. But then we began to remember back farther.

"Do you remember our tenth anniversary?" I asked. "We lived south of Sidney and then had our three little boys. They stayed with your parents in Sidney, and we went down to St. Joseph, Missouri, where we spent our wedding night and tried to retrace our steps. We went to the dinner-dance place on the main highway of that day and had dinner and danced. I had made a new organdy dress to wear and felt very glamorous that night."

"We went clear down to Eureka Springs, Arkansas, on one of our anniversaries. Went out to Lake Lucerne where we had a cabin for several nights and that was good to retrace those steps as well.

"We went back again two years ago with Jeff to find that Lake Lucerne was still there. And we stayed in the old Basin Park Hotel in Eureka Springs, Arkansas, where we had stayed on our honeymoon."

"Where were we on our fiftieth?" Robert asked.

"Oh, that's a real easy one." I said, "The boys took us to the Empress Hotel in Victoria, British Columbia, for that celebration. We had high tea, and dinner in the elegant hotel dining room and went to a symphony concert. Then, later in the week, we went up to one of the nearby islands for several nights in a cabin back in the woods "

"Any other memorable ones?" Robert asked.

"How about our fifty-fourth anniversary when we were with our family on the Mississippi Queen paddle boat going up the Ohio River? The most memorable ones are when we are all together."

Then we remembered that some years we do nothing special, maybe buy a steak, put a pretty cloth on the table, bring out the calla lily candles from our wedding reception, and wish each other many more memorable years and anniversaries together.

Spreading My Wings

Here I am standing by my Iowa Walk of Fame tile embedded in the Shenandoah sidewalk, June 6, 2009. Robert and I in the back, grandchildren Nick and Amanda in the front. Photo by the children's father, Craig Birkby.

Leanna and Me

THE SUN WAS SHINING brightly into the lovely sunroom that afternoon in 1955. I waited with anticipation while the person I had come to see completed her telephone conversation. Books filled the shelves in one portion of the room, flowers bloomed on the windowsill and spilled over the pots along the wall, and a partially finished hooked rug lay over a chair arm. It took very little imagination to know the type of person who lived in this attractive home.

Glancing through a door to the north of the sunroom, I could see a desk with a microphone surrounded by letters, clippings, and recipes for the next day's broadcasting. A corner of a bedroom, convenient and homey, was visible next to the broadcast room. The handmade quilt on the bed was one of many I was to see in the years ahead.

While I waited and enjoyed the sunshine pouring in through the large windows, my mind went back to the first time I had heard the voice of the person I had come to see, Leanna Driftmier. It was in 1936 when my family moved to Sidney, Iowa, that I became aware of the *Kitchen-Klatter* program and listened to Leanna as she brought her daily visit over the radio. My mother listened, and she also read the *Kitchen-Klatter Magazine*, finding useful household hints, trying the recipes, and appreciating the friendly visits.

I listened, enjoyed eating the food Mother prepared from Kitchen-Klatter recipes, and found it amazing to know a family as well as we came to know the Driftmiers and their activities. Just as others who have listened to the program and read the magazine have said many, many times, they became like next-door neighbors. It was not until later when I married and returned to the Shenandoah area that I truly realized the strength and value of Leanna's sharing of her life with me. So often, her helpful hints would solve problems I didn't even know I had. After we had our first baby and moved near Ames so Robert could attend Iowa State College, Leanna's cheerful voice would make my day less lonely. It meant a great deal to a new mother so far from relatives and friends to hear that familiar voice bringing guidance and assistance. Leanna's visits became a daily part of my life.

When we moved to the farm, Leanna came along. When we had more children, Leanna helped raise them just as she had our first. She helped me with gardening, canning, and house cleaning, through dull days and bright.

For several years I also had a daily radio program over at KMA, and our paths finally crossed when I met Leanna for the first time at a gathering of radio homemakers.

And now, with the phone conversation completed, Leanna wheeled into the sunroom to interrupt my reminiscing. She asked about my family and commented on the column I had been writing for almost five years in the *Shenandoah Evening Sentinel*. She told me she had enjoyed reading my articles and had invited me to come to her house for the purpose of asking me to write a feature article each month for the *Kitchen-Klatter Magazine*.

Leanna has a way of making a person feel like they can do anything. Her arguments were convincing. Her loving, friendly manner left me no doubt that I wanted to be a part of the *Kitchen-Klatter* family.

Leanna continued to guide me as I began writing for the magazine. Bob was five and just starting kindergarten. Jeff was one year old, and our new baby Craig arrived the following December. Leanna gave me far more than I ever gave her in the way of assistance.

Several months later, Leanna decided to go to California and leave daughters Lucile and Margery in charge of the broadcasting for a time. Suddenly, Lucile was faced with unexpected surgery. Remembering that I had done radio work, Lucile called to see if I could fill in with sister Margery while she was in the hospital. The broadcasting was done in Leanna's home, so that first broadcast in February of 1956 was from the small room just around the corner from the sunroom where Leanna and I had enjoyed our talk about my writing for the magazine. It was with a feeling of awe that I began the first broadcast; this was the very room where so many of the visits had originated which I had heard as a girl, as a young wife, and as a mother. Somehow it gave the sensation of a fairy tale come true.

As time went on, I was called to broadcast when needed. It has been a happy association since it gave me more time for my growing family than full-time work would have. It was exciting when I was on the air with Leanna, for I have long appreciated her ready wit, her refreshing laugh, her cheerful approach to all of life's problems, and our shared interests.

Life brings about strange circumstances. My move to southwest Iowa brought Leanna to my attention. Early writing and broadcasting experiences brought me to Leanna's attention, and once we got together, it became a lasting friendship which continued for over twenty years until Leanna passed away in 1976. But even with her departure, I often feel her presence when I write my columns or do my broadcasts.

Michael and Jane Stern

IT WAS COMPLETELY accidental that I came to the attention of food writers Jane and Michael Stern.

I had been working for radio station KMA and for *Kitchen-Klatter* for several years when I began to collect material on the stories of the radio homemakers. I realized that I had some interesting stories about some amazing women, so I wrote to the editorial department of the *Des Moines Register*, Iowa's premier newspaper. I told them I had these stories and would like to write an article for their paper.

"No," they answered back. "We think you have a great idea but we want one of our staff writers to research and write it. We'll send someone down to Shenandoah to interview you."

Well! I was not pleased. After all, this was my story. But soon I grew calmer and realized that I had a story that was too important to be pushed aside. I told the editors to send their reporter down and I would do whatever I could to help. So it came to pass that a story of the radio homemakers was written for the *Des Moines Register* and in the body of the article I was listed as the story consultant.

It so happened that a young woman named Susan Puckett was attending Iowa State College in Ames at this time, and she was writing a cookbook entitled *A Cook's Tour of Iowa* to be published by the University of Iowa Press. She saw the newspaper article about the radio homemakers and found my name as the consultant and called me. She wanted to put a chapter in her book about the radio homemakers with some of their recipes. I was delighted.

It also turned out that Susan and national known food writers Michael and Jane Stern were friends. So it was through her that the Sterns found me and out they came to Iowa to find out what all this excitement about the radio homemakers was about. They stayed for a long weekend interviewing radio personalities, longtime listeners, KMA personnel, and going out into the Iowa countryside to get a feel for the beauty of the area. They ate meals on my screened-in porch—a fine breakfast, two teas with neighbors, and one memorable dinner with the best Iowa foods I could conjure up from our garden and in my kitchen.

When they went back to their home in Connecticut, Jane and Michael Stern wrote a twelve-page article about their trip to southwest Iowa for the *New Yorker* magazine. That opened up doors I never dreamed of in my simple rural Iowa life. All three national television stations came calling, and several came to southwest Iowa to film for their news programs. I went to Washington, D.C., where I did an hour on *Night Watch* (with Karen Ann Falk, radio homemaker Florence Falk's daughter). I flew to New York for a Fourth of July food program on CBS with Hattie Kaufman as my moderator. I also appeared on the Peter Jennings show on ABC with its film crew, who came out to my house and other southwest Iowa locations. In between were National Public Radio and PBS with interviews that were delightful to do.

Jane and Michael continue to get mileage out of the meal they had on our porch. They wrote a delightful introduction for my *Up A Country Lane* book, later put my stories in their *Road Food* books, and in September 2010 they had an article in *Saveur Magazine* called "Neighboring" that included on the cover a photo of the main dish from that memorable Iowa meal, Virginia Miller's Elegant Pork Chops.

So here is the recipe that impressed the two food writers to keep using it in their publications. It is one of the two recipes I have included in three of my books.

Virginia Miller's Elegant Pork Chops

4 double-cut, bone-in pork chops
Salt and pepper, to taste
1⅓ cups water
2 cups brown sugar
2 cups soy sauce
1 tablespoon molasses
1¾ cups ketchup
1½ cups chili sauce, such as Heinz
2 tablespoons French dressing
1 tablespoon dry mustard

Put pork chops into a baking dish and season with salt and pepper. In a small bowl, whisk ½ cup brown sugar, soy sauce, molasses, and 1 cup water and pour over meat. Cover with plastic wrap and let pork chops marinate in the refrigerator for at least 4 hours. Heat oven to 375 degrees. Drain pork chops and transfer to a 9 × 13-inch baking dish. Whisk together remaining brown sugar, ketchup, chili sauce, French dressing, mustard, and ⅓ cup water in a small bowl. Pour sauce over pork chops and bake, turning pork chops and basting with sauce occasionally, until pork chops are tender and sauce has thickened, about 45 minutes. Let pork chops rest for 10 minutes before serving. Serves 4.

My Friendship with Fannie Flagg

IT WAS A BRIGHT, SUNNY Iowa spring day when the telephone rang, and I picked it up to say "Hello," little realizing what an interesting new friend was reaching out to me.

"Hello," a familiar voice said. I could not place it exactly, so I was surprised when the voice continued by saying, "This is Fannie Flagg."

"*Oh my*," I answered, "I only know one Fannie Flagg in the entire world."

"That's me. I found your book *Neighboring on the Air* in a little book store in Georgia, bought it, took it home and read it, and was entranced by the stories of the radio homemakers. I would like to develop a character based on these women in my next book and would like you to help me with the research. Would you be willing to do so?"

"I would be very happy to help you in any way I can." Thus began a most interesting experience. Fannie would ask me questions, and I would either know the answers or find them for her. Such as, "What did the radio homemakers' homes look like? Can you outline the floor plans of their houses for me? Did the ladies have easygoing or wiry, tense personalities? What were their families like?" and on and on. "I have the stories from your book that tell how they became radio homemakers," said Fannie, "and those are very helpful as I put together my character of 'Neighbor Dorothy.'"

And Fannie fashioned her fictional radio homemaker to her liking and introduced her in the book *Welcome to the World, Baby Girl!*

But her fascination with radio homemakers didn't stop there. Her next book was *Standing in the Rainbow,* and the main character was Neighbor Dorothy, a radio homemaker. In one portion of the book, she even has Neighbor Dorothy go from her home in Missouri up to Shenandoah, Iowa, to station KMA—"Dorothy was up in Iowa that weekend to visit with her friend and fellow radio homemaker Evelyn Birkby and to participate in the big home-demonstration show at the Mayfair Auditorium in Shenandoah," Fannie wrote.

Fannie continued with the character in her delightful book *Can't Wait to Get to Heaven.* Dorothy's Aunt Elner goes to heaven, and while she is there, she has a visit with Neighbor Dorothy, who bakes a cake for her. How typical of a radio homemaker to continue cooking even in heaven.

Did I ever meet Fannie Flagg in person? Indeed I did.

She was scheduled to do a book signing of *Standing in the Rainbow* in Kansas City and she invited me to come down from my home in Sidney, Iowa, to meet her there. The event was sponsored by a local bookstore and held in the Community Christian Church, which was designed by Frank Lloyd Wright, a perfect setting for a memorable event.

Son Craig was home that weekend and so went with Robert and me to discover a large group of over two hundred Fannie Flagg fans gathered in the auditorium. Fannie, who had visited with me for a time before the presentation, enthralled the audience with her wry wit and her delightful stories of writing the book. She told them of the way she found me—a real live radio homemaker—and asked me to be her consultant. And then she asked me to visit with the folks about how all of this came about.

I can say without question that it was one of the most event-filled evenings of my life, for the people who attended were some of the most attentive, complimentary, and encouraging I had ever experienced. Following the speeches, Fannie invited me to autograph and sell my books along with her. We concluded the evening with a friendship that has continued to this day.

Iowa Public Television Comes Calling

FOR THE PAST YEAR the talented professionals of Iowa Public Television have been putting together a documentary entitled *Iowa's Radio Homemakers: Up a Country Lane*.

Director Deb Herbold recently came to Sidney with a preview copy of the completed documentary to share with Robert and me.

Before watching the program, we took Deb to Penn Drug to enjoy sandwiches for lunch. As we ate, I asked her how she happened to come up with the idea of the documentary.

"I was doing research on another project at the Iowa Women's Archives in Iowa City and I ran across your picture," she explained. "It said you were, among other things, a radio homemaker, and I had no idea what a radio homemaker was, so I decided to find out."

She read a copy of my *Up a Country Lane Cookbook* and became fascinated with stories of Iowa farm life in the 1940s and 1950s. Eager to learn more, she put together a plan for a documentary television program, pitched it to Iowa Public Television, and got a very positive response.

I asked Deb about the challenges of developing the documentary.

"The hardest part was blending two stories together," she explained. "One story is about what life was like in this region in the 1940s and 1950s. Woven into that is the story of the radio homemakers."

She told me that she very much enjoyed visiting with the people she interviewed. So many of my dear friends took part—Chuck Offenburger, Tom Morain, Emily Bengtson, Marilyn Benson, and quite a few others.

"I didn't know about country social clubs," Deb told me when I asked what surprised her in her research. "I found the stories fascinating about the way the farm women got together once or twice a month to socialize, catch up on the news of the community, and share recipes."

Deb contacted me a year ago to begin exploring the impact of the radio homemakers. "Radio homemaking sounds so simple," she recalled, "but I learned that you women were encouraging influences in the lives of many people who lived in isolated areas of the Midwest."

After lunch we took Deb to our home to preview the documentary. Twenty-seven hours of taping had been edited down to an hour-long program, plus a second DVD of outtake scenes and stories Deb felt were important to preserve.

It was so exciting to sit with her in our family room and watch the television program unfold. Deb told me she wanted to be with me the first time I saw the documentary, and I'm sure that my exclamations, comments, and even a few tears did not disappoint her.

As Deb drove away down our snow-packed lane, I thought of how many moments of Iowa life she has documented on film. I hope the program will be a gift of memory for many who lived here during the 1940s and 1950s, and for their children and grandchildren who have heard so many stories about those remarkable bygone days.

Shenandoah's Walk of Fame

THE IDEA OF enshrining famous people in cement along a city's sidewalks is not unusual for Hollywood but is somewhat unique in Iowa. Today the town of Shenandoah has over 125 Iowa-shaped sidewalk plaques located along its main business streets paying tribute to famous Iowans.

So it was that I was chosen both to be one of the honorees and also to give the keynote speech at the June 6, 2009, dedication of the people newly embedded in the Shenandoah Walk of Fame. On a lovely

June day a large crowd gathered for the event in downtown Shenandoah around the old WCTU fountain and the flatiron building.

This is what I said that day:

I thank you for including me in this year's walk of fame. My thanks to Lee Kingery, who first had the vision for this project, to the rest of the committee and to all of you who came today. I especially want to recognize my fellow honorees—I read Laura Ingalls Wilder's books as I was growing up. Robert and I stayed in the Ally Oop room in the turn-of-the-century hotel in Perry, Iowa, so we know about him. Bill Leacox was a contemporary of my son Bob, and now he is a nationally known musician. Robert and I listen to Lawrence Welk's programs even today, so we enjoy Dick Dale of Algona, Iowa, Singer and Musician, one of today's honorees. It is an amazing group of special people who are being honored today in the Walk of Fame.

The first time I remember being in Shenandoah was in the fall of 1935. My family had moved to Sidney that year, and my minister father was invited by Henry Field to come to his studio to preach over radio station KFNF. Dad was told he could bring some musicians along if he wished and he wished for my sister Ruth, who played the guitar, and me. Calling us musicians was a stretch—but we knew the old church hymns from memory and sang heartily to make up for any lack of quality. Surprisingly, we were invited back. Does this mean I can say I started my radio career seventy-four years ago at the age of fifteen at KFNF?

That began my love affair with Shenandoah but little did I realize the role this community would play in my life.

Now, as I walk down the street of this city and look at the names on the Iowa map outlines embedded in cement, I imagine I hear the voices of those who have meant so much in my life and to the lives of everyone in this area.

The one whose booming voice cast a wide swath across the landscape, and determined much of my future was *Evening Sentinel* publisher Willard Archie. He gave me the opportunity to try writing a weekly newspaper column in 1949, and that allowed me to come into your homes via newspapers.

It was the recipes that almost did me in—"Put in a recipe every week," Mr. Archie directed. What Mr. Archie didn't know is that I couldn't cook! I began a collection of recipes from neighbors, friends, and relatives that turned me into a reasonable cook and eventually an author of cookbooks. Soon following the advent of my column, Doris Murphy, Women's Director for KMA radio, asked me to be one of their radio homemakers. Because you let me share your lives, I began sharing mine with you.

Ed May, Frank Field, Andy Anderson, and my mentors Doris Murphy, Bernice Currier, Adella Shoemaker, Edythe Sterlin, Edith Hansen, Billie Oakley, and dear Leanna Driftmier, who first invited me to be a part of the *Kitchen-Klatter Magazine* and radio work, were my contemporaries.

These special people helped make Shenandoah what it is today—and many of them have their names already in the Walk of Fame. I feel very humble to be included with their names. Like the movie stars in the walk in front of the Grauman's Chinese Theatre, I am delighted to have this happen when I could be here in person. Sadly, many of those whose names are here left us before they knew this event was going to happen. I am glad to be alive and well and able to share the honor today with them and have my husband Robert and son Bob here representing my family who gave me support and encouragement and subjects to write about.

Sharing my life is something I plan to do for the rest of my days, grateful for your love and concern. Southwest Iowa is a place to treasure, to preserve, to keep that spirit of neighborliness alive, and to understand the value of this special place. There is no other place like it on earth.

I accept this Walk of Fame honor with joy—thank you for making me a part of this celebration.

A Gaggle of Radio Homemakers

THE TELEPHONE CALL from Dr. Steve Smethers at Kansas State University's School of Journalism and Mass Communications was a surprise. He called to ask me to come to KSU and participate in the fifth annual Great Plains Radio History Symposium.

"There is a perception that radio was a creation of the East and West Coasts, and that's not completely the case," he explained. "There is rich history of radio in the Central Plains where lots of programming was directed to the farm and home."

The 2010 symposium would include a focus on women. Dr. Smethers asked if I would speak on the panel for "Homemaking Programs: Radio's Recipe for Attracting Women Listeners." I wholeheartedly agreed to come.

Last week the university sent Jeff Rake, a young journalism student, to drive me from my home in southwest Iowa to Manhattan, Kansas. I enjoyed visiting with him as we traveled across the beautiful midwestern countryside. Once we reached the school, Jeff arranged for me to tour the KSU campus. I was impressed by the wonderful limestone buildings, first constructed in 1861.

After a restful night at a hotel near the university, I found my way to the student union and joined a panel before a gathering of a hundred people interested in radio and women's role in broadcasting through the years. Dr. Smethers was our moderator, and I enjoyed sharing memories with others on the panel.

Seated with me was Deanne Wright, who explained that her inspiration to be a broadcast journalist came from her mother, Ona Belle Phillips. Ona Belle had hosted a daily news program over KJCK Radio in Junction City, Kansas. Deanne remembered that for a time, her mother had broadcast from a makeshift studio in the family home.

Deanne majored in journalism at the University of Kansas, then received master's degrees from Kansas State University in journalism and mass communications. In 1971 she became KSAC Radio's "women's director." Her title later changed to "family living director" and her program evolved from recipes and sewing tips to a content exploring economics, parenting advice, and other issues that reflected the reality of raising a family.

The other member of our panel was Vernadell Yarrow, whose women's program aired over a small radio station that covered just thirty miles of Kansas farmland. She and her husband Larry ran a family farm south of Clay Center where they raised three children. That background gave her plenty of material when she started a program called *Coffee Time* that featured recipes, household hints, and folksy chats, the hallmarks of early radio homemakers. The program was so successful that she began hosting a second show, *Tea Time*, highlighting community events.

Our two-hour panel discussion covered a wide range of topics about women in broadcasting. We shared stories about our beginnings in radio, our listeners, and how we addressed the needs of our audiences.

The program concluded with Dr. Smethers asking, "Why does this history matter? I tell our students we need to appreciate the pioneering journalists and broadcasters who played such important roles in shaping our rural culture."

Before we went our separate ways, Kansas Public Radio interviewed the panel members, inviting us to elaborate on our thoughts about midwestern radio history. Then it was time for lunch and the three-hour drive back to Sidney.

My driver this time was Kristie Russell, another delightful journalism student. I enjoyed our conversation as we motored across northeast Kansas, a bit of Nebraska, and into Iowa. When I saw the Loess Hills ahead, I knew I was almost home.

It was a delightful experience. I came away with new friends and the assurance that the history of radio and the place of women broadcasters is being well preserved.

Simpson College, My Alma Mater

BILL FRIEDRICKS IS HEAD of the history department at Simpson College in Indianola, Iowa. For three years he has been trying to arrange a time when I could come to the campus to be a part of the History Lecture Series. Finally, on a rainy March day, our son Jeff arrived from his home in Montana just in time to drive Robert and me to Des Moines to the Simpson College Des Moines campus for its March history event.

After all these years of trying, I finally met Bill, with his great smile, his enthusiasm for history, and his delight in the college from which I "graduated" in 1938, following a two-year education course.

"Come and tell us what it was like to be a college student in the 1930s," was part of the invitation, "and how your career developed through the years."

So there we were, in the lovely atrium of the building where Simpson has its extended classes with a wonderful group of people of all ages—some old friends (including Brenda Kay McConahay, a former KMA radio homemaker who now lives in Des Moines), Simpson students, and history buffs of all ages.

I told them of my two years on campus and how different it was then, for it was the depth of the Great Depression. I rented a room in a private home, sharing the room and the bed with a fellow student for $9 a month. This included cooking privileges. My food bill was $1 a week plus the food my mother sent me from home. I watched the sales and bought three-cent dented cans of vegetables, ten-cent slices of meat, and a pound of coffee for seventeen cents. I worked to augment my income, baby-sitting for twenty-five cents an evening, and I worked in sorority house kitchens doing dishes and ironing for ten cents an hour. It was a happy time, for I was fortunate to be able to come to college at all.

The Simpson College campus was much smaller when I was a student in the 1930s than it is today. The small fine arts building was then the library. The elegant old chapel building, newly remodeled into lovely meeting rooms, had a third floor that was a large assembly hall. Chapel was held in this large third-floor room three times a week, and all students were required to attend. I remember it as being very drab with dark brown wood surrounding all the walls. I came in to this Methodist-related college during a "reserved" period—no smoking, drinking, or card-playing were allowed, and my freshman year was the first time they allowed dancing in their gymnasium. I was happy to receive my State of Iowa teaching certificate at the end of the two years, little realizing how helpful that education would be to me through my life.

An education background can help with everything a person does. The years I taught in Iowa led to my work as Director of Religious Education in Grace Methodist Church in Waterloo, Iowa. "I would never have been hired in that position without an education background, for the basis of any teaching—be it public or religious—is the same."

Then I got to the place in my story where I was married and lived on a small farm south of Farragut and started writing for the *Shenandoah Evening Sentinel* and, soon after, broadcasting on KMA. Again, I gave credit to Simpson for the knowledge and experience they had given me that gave me confidence to try those new tasks.

History comes in many forms—dates, battles, government—but the stories of people and what happens to them is, to me, the most interesting and important part of history. And as I look back over my history, it seems evident that the two years I spent at Simpson College had a profound effect on everything I have done all these years since.

It was a delight to share my college stories with current Simpson students and others interested in early Simpson history.

As we drove back to our Des Moines hotel following the evening presentation, a heavy white snow was falling fast. What I hoped was Iowa's last snowstorm of the season had descended upon us. As we turned into the entrance to our hotel, we decided to stay in Des Moines the next day and wait out the storm before returning to Sidney. That extra day in Des Moines allowed me to bathe in the memories of my Simpson College years for a bit more before returning home.

Aging Is an Opportunity

It Is What It Is

ROBERT AND I HAVE JUST returned from having our yearly physical checkups at the doctor's office. Nothing makes me feel more like my chronological age than such a visit, although the doctor told Robert, who is almost ninety-three and me, now ninety-two, that we are in much better shape than most people our age.

I don't know what people our age are supposed to be like, but I do know that we are fortunate to be in the shape we are in. Even so, there are times when I would agree with a description of old age I heard from an elderly person recently: "I have too many faulty parts and too much old."

I watch as Robert walks across the yard and climbs onto the riding lawnmower to do one of his favorite activities—mow. It is good he likes to do this task and is able to do it, for he has several acres to cover. He tells me he likes to mow because he can do a lot of thinking as he gets some work done, and I'm sure that's true.

His walk is becoming slower and his shoulders more stooped. He shuffles a bit as he goes, and getting up from a chair is more difficult. As an early Father's Day gift, Craig gave his dad one of those chairs that lifts him nearly to his feet and all but kicks him out. We laugh about it being a "catapult chair," but it has certainly been a help.

Robert is also struggling with arthritic knees. I wonder how many ninety-year-olds have arthritis in one joint or another, and if there are any who don't. My finger joints are showing the effect of that ailment, too.

My mother and my sister had severe arthritis that was also painful. While my hands have become a bit lumpy, I am so grateful there's little pain. I had a gimpy shoulder, but putting a small pillow under that aggravated joint while I slept has given relief. We make adjustments.

Robert's recent bout with pneumonia really slowed him down and we are hoping that he soon regains his lost energy. The doctor has told him to be patient, that even after getting over the illness, full recovery can take several more months. "And stay off ladders," the physician continued. "I have too many older folks who have been badly hurt falling off of ladders."

I'm grateful that my mind is still sharp, though I have a theory that we keep piling information into our minds as the years go by, and eventually our heads get stuffed full. At least that's my excuse when I can't find a word or a name quickly. My recent addition of a pacemaker to help keep my heart beating at a proper rate has helped sharpen my mind noticeably.

Robert and I both concentrate on all the positive, good things that are happening in our lives. We have the great joy of sharing many experiences with our grown children and two wonderful grandchildren. Friends and neighbors are very dear to us, and we appreciate all the time we can spend with them.

Speaking of friends, one challenge of old age is seeing most of our generation passing away ahead of us. When I go to Simpson College reunions, I am the last remaining graduate of my class.

The Sidney High School alumni events include fewer and fewer of our classmates. We remember them all with great fondness but are sad they are no longer around.

One rule I have for myself is that if someone offers help, I accept it. I have seen too many people who, as they become less able to do activities, become resentful and refuse assistance as a way to declare their independence. If someone opens a door or wants to help me up some steps, I thank them for their kindness and take it as an opportunity to begin a conversation.

Growing old is what it is. There's no getting around it. Parts will become faulty and old will gradually become too much. Meanwhile, we are in 2011. We will celebrate the time we have, just as we have at every stage of life, and approach each day with enthusiasm and joy.

Too Old to Be Elderly

I DISCOVERED the other day that, much to my surprise, I am too old to be an elderly person. The occasion was a very delightful visit with Kara Cruickshank.

She is the daughter of Lynda and Gregg Cruickshank of Sidney and is a student at the University of Nebraska, Lincoln, majoring in family science and minoring in gerontology and psychology.

For an assignment for her gerontology class, she was to find and interview several elderly persons. The assignment defined elderly as "someone between the ages of 65 and 85." I told Kara that here I am in 2011 at the age of ninety-two, so sadly I didn't qualify to be elderly. She laughed as she assured me it was okay. She would squeeze me in.

I brought out hot tea and shortbread cookies to nourish us while we talked, and we launched into our visit with Kara's first question.

"If you could give the current college students advice, what would it be?"

I was asked the same question when I spoke last week at a Simpson College event, so I had the answer ready.

"First, I would tell them to keep their minds sharp," I explained. "Stay away from drugs and cigarettes, too much alcohol. A person only gets one mind in a lifetime, and those fortunate enough to live a long time will be very glad they kept their minds sharp."

"Secondly," I told her, "stay positive. Too many people spend their lives being negative, critical, and complaining. Being happy is much healthier.

"Third, drink lots of milk."

Kara asked me to talk about what I considered the hardest part of my earlier days. I remember that time was much more labor intensive. As a young mother, for example, I used a wringer washer that required much manual effort. Then I hung all the clothes outdoors on a clothesline to dry.

Mondays were usually wash day, and it took most of the day to get the laundry done. Much of Tuesday was devoted to doing the ironing.

"What for you was the most memorable event of the last century?" Kara asked. "The communication revolution," I told her. "The computer has made my work so much easier."

I explained that I wrote my newspaper column for thirty-five years on a big Royal typewriter. I used carbon paper to make a copy as I typed, then mailed the original to the newspaper in Shenandoah. In 1985 I bought my first computer, a 512K MacIntosh. It had a very big monitor and a very small screen, but I didn't need carbon paper anymore. I would copy my column onto a disc and mail that.

Today with the internet, I write my column on my Leopard big screen computer, use the spell-checker, then hit the *send* button and email my column to the *Valley News*. I also keep my website up to date and have even started sharing postings on Facebook.

I poured Kara some more tea and had a cookie while I waited for her next question. It was very interesting coming from someone so young. "Do you like growing old?" she asked.

I thought a moment before I replied.

"Each year offers something new and exciting and challenging," I explained. "I've had so many opportunities in my life to be involved with wonderful people and interesting work."

I told her about the satisfaction I'd experienced starting children's choirs in churches where none had existed before and helping launch youth and young adult groups from scratch. My column has been a joy since 1949, when publisher Willard Archie decided the *Shenandoah Evening Sentinel* needed one.

"As long as I keep looking for them, new opportunities keep appearing," I concluded. "Every age has its special pleasures and opportunities, even after ninety."

As one of her final questions, Kara asked me what I look forward to in the future. I could answer that one without hesitation.

"Watching my sons as they continue to expand their careers and my grandchildren as they grow into fine young people," I said. "I look forward to completing my current project, a book that will be a collection of my favorite columns. And I treasure every day with Robert, my husband of sixty-five years."

Before she left, Kara promised to send me a copy of her paper and let me know what grade she received for her efforts (she got an A+). I wished her well and told her I hoped her search would give her assurance that old age is something to look forward to. Aging is an opportunity, not something to fear.

Facebook—The Modern Hollow Tree

MY COLLEGE psychology teacher, back in the 1940s, imprinted me with certain information.

For example, I still remember what he said were some basic needs for every person's life:

Security
Recognition
New experiences
Love

I currently have all of these needs fulfilled in my life in comfortable quantities, though I'm eager for more new experiences to come. They are coming along a bit more infrequently than they have in the past.

I decided just as I reached my ninetieth birthday at the end of July 2009 that it was time to try something new—Facebook.

I had heard a lot about Facebook, and it sounded fascinating. I'd been told it was a social networking way to connect with friends and relatives and make new friends. It is an opportunity to expand my experiences, and at least for now, it should satisfy having a new experience in my life.

When our son Jeff was home for a visit recently, he helped set up a Facebook page for me. Everything operated fine while he was here, but then he returned to his home in Montana and left me pretty uneducated about the process of using this new technology.

That has been a new experience, too, as I am learning how to manage and enjoy Facebook on my own. People check in and leave messages of what is going on in their lives, and then they comment on items others have posted about their lives.

It reminds me of pioneer days before regular mail delivery came to people's homes. Some would leave notes in hollow trees for their neighbors to find. The neighbors would return the favor with notes of their own.

Facebook is like the old tree with the hollow in it. I open my page and there are all kinds of interesting notes from people I enjoy hearing from and about.

I realize that what little I am doing so far with online social networking is just the tip of the iceberg. Once I get Facebook mastered, will I want to go on to Twitter and blogging and all the other new internet social networking sites? Time will tell.

Meanwhile, Jeff has ventured out into a new internet experience of his own. For the next three months he is hosting *Sustainable Agriculture Spotlight,* an hour-long weekly radio program on *Voice America* that focuses on sustainable agriculture.

It's a new type of radio show that is only broadcast over the internet, so I can listen to it any time I want through my computer instead of through the radio.

On his radio broadcast Jeff has been interviewing national experts on topics including building greenhouses, making biodiesel fuel on the farm, and raising organic livestock. For over twenty years, Jeff has been working for the National Center for Appropriate Technology (NCAT), a nonprofit organization promoting sustainable agriculture and renewable energy projects for state and federal agencies.

I am always fascinated when he tells us about what he is doing, and his radio program catches my imagination in the same way. All of his hour-long broadcasts are archived online on the Green Talk Network on *Voice America*.

One day Jeff suggested that I broadcast with him on his radio program in August when I'm in Montana. I have gladly accepted his offer. Since his internet radio program is focused on sustainable farming and agriculture, I will talk about farm life in rural Iowa in the 1940s and 1950s.

Life continues to bring new opportunities. Now I have the opportunity to become more computer savvy. I think I'm doing pretty well to be coming up on my ninetieth year and have my own website, a Facebook page, and to be interviewed on my son's online radio program!

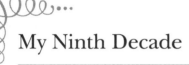

My Ninth Decade

AS I TURN THE CALENDAR to January of 2010, I am reminded it is time for me to take a few moments and look back on the decade we've just completed, my ninth.

Ten years ago when we reached the year 2000, I was excited to move into a fresh new year and a brand new century. We celebrated that night with friends Chuck and Carla Offenburger, rang the church bells, and had high hopes for years to come, full of peace and prosperity.

The first challenge was the Y2K computer glitch scare when people feared all computers would shut down because they weren't programmed to deal with the digits of the new century. That proved to be nothing, but then came 9/11 and the war that followed.

I wrote several columns about my concern, pleading for other solutions besides killing. The economic depression came too, compared by some to the Great Depression of my childhood. Now at the end of

2009 it is supposed to be easing. I hope we are making progress, both with the economy and the ongoing conflicts abroad.

In political matters, I've felt we have made progress in the variety of those in public office. Women are being taken seriously as candidates, and we now live in an age when an African American can be elected president.

The past decade has been a good one for our family. Our son Craig and his wife Sharon added Amanda Mae Birkby to the family and older son Nick is maturing into a fine young man. Craig's Seattle Skin Cancer Center continued to expand and he completed his ten-thousandth surgery there this past month.

After a sabbatical for full-time motherhood, Craig's wife Sharon has returned to her clinic two days a week to care for her own dermatology patients.

A highlight of son Jeff's decade was his move from Butte, Montana, to Missoula, where he threw his energies into restoring a snug little bungalow for his home. He continues to work as a senior staff member for the National Center for Appropriate Technology, spreading information about renewable energy, sustainable communities, and environmentally appropriate methods of agriculture.

His work includes conducting radio broadcasts with guests and discussing current and future environmental efforts. I was very pleased the day he invited me to join him on one of his programs.

Bob continues to have outdoor adventures and write books about his experiences. His latest is his third edition of the *Boy Scout Handbook*, this one commemorating the organization's one-hundredth anniversary.

Mountain Madness, his book about his mountaineering friend Scott Fischer, received favorable reviews in the *New York Times*. His most recent explorations have taken him several times to Siberia, where he is helping young Russians learn how to construct hiking trails in their national parks.

Robert and I continue to enjoy our home on Honey Hill and the routine that has continued over the last ten years. He gets up every morning, eager to get busy with the many tasks of working in the yard, delivering Meals on Wheels, and helping out with the church, the Historical society, and the Masonic Lodge.

We both feel very fortunate that we can continue to travel to visit loved ones, both near and far away. In recent years Robert's nephew, Larry Barnard, and his wife Diane moved to Sidney and have become an important part of our lives.

My own daily routine continues to revolve around my family and my writing. The concluding year of the last decade, 2009, was an eventful one for me. I celebrated my nintieth birthday, the sixtieth anniversary of writing my weekly column, plus recognizing it had been sixty years ago that I did my first radio broadcast. I continue to be on the air once a month with radio station KMA in Shenandoah, Iowa.

On top of the piano in my study is my old Royal typewriter that was my daily companion through the early decades of my writing. I still use it some to type address labels, but on my desk is my primary helper, a gleaming updated Apple computer.

It is the fifth computer I've owned in the last two decades, and I am pleased I've been able to keep up with the basic technologies. Several years ago I even launched a website, and while I recently started a Facebook page, I still have much to learn before that becomes a natural part of the way I communicate with others. But I feel a part of cyberspace, and welcome it into my life.

Robert and I celebrated our sixty-third wedding anniversary, grateful to still be together. We enjoyed many family gatherings here in Sidney, in Montana, and in Washington State. I was delighted to be honored by being included in Shenandoah, Iowa's special Walk of Fame.

Now, as I move into my tenth decade of life, I wish for much that I have wished for in every other decade. I hope for a world with fewer wars and greater understanding of one another. I wish for everyone the joy of satisfying lives full of family, fun, and friendship. And I look forward to the coming years with enthusiasm and hope.